IT'S TIME TO
INSPIRE!

IT'S TIME TO INSPIRE!

How to Stop Looking for Role Models and be One Instead in 9 simple steps

Authored by

SHRIDHAR AIYER

penmanbooks.com

Penman Books

Office No. 303, Kumar House Building,
D Block, Central Market, Opp PVR Cinema,
Prashant Vihar, Delhi 110085, India
Website: www.penmanbooks.com
Email: publish@penmanbooks.com

Published by Penman Books 2019

Title: It's Time to Inspire!
Price: ₹270 | $11.99
ISBN: 978-93-57844-05-5

"The man who moves a mountain begins by carrying away small stones."

—Confucius China.551 BC

Acknowledgments

Among the more spoken of clichés of our times is the notion, that an author's life is full of retreating to a corner to write, and that his ideas spring from a mystical inner self and that he writes somehow, under the spell of that inspiration. Most first time authors like me know otherwise. Writing a book is much harder than I thought and more rewarding than I imagined. The experience is challenging but gratifying in the end. ***It's time to inspire*** is a product of gregarious, face to face and mind to mind contact with dozens of individuals from corporate and different universities and countries that it would be impossible for me to list them all.

I am thankful to all those who have been an influence for this book and who have persuaded me to clarify and integrate the concepts on which this book is based, and whom I have had the opportunity to meet or see from far. They have taught me to see life from a surprisingly fresh perspective. I also want to thank some wonderful people who I met at some turns of life who said some really positive things and taught me to be strong like Hercules. I heard all of you and it meant something.

To my family and best friends who have more faith and belief in me than I do, and love me for what I am and remind me of what I truly can be, from time to time. This book is in large measure, their book as well as mine. You know who you are. Thank you!

This book is also dedicated to the elements of Curiosity within all of us and how that separates the truly alive from the rest.

Be courageous… Be Curious!

Foreword

This is a book about what happens if you only think of following and never to lead and the impact it has on the social consciousness of the society we live in today. Much has been written about inspiration. Yet for the most part, books on inspiration have a slightly clinical tone. These pages, by contrast, concern themselves with the humane side of leadership and inspiring others. Moreover, they concern themselves with the steps by which we are likely to do just that. They deal with everyday happenings and events, the places that we leave behind, the places we work at and the people who pass through our lives with crazy speeds. The future of leadership and humanities is probed along with the present prodded for good measure.

What joins all of this, in this book, as it does in life, is the huge current of change that threatens to envelop us all. This current is so powerful that it overturns corporate institutions, questions our values and moves our roots. This book argues with force, hopefully, that, unless we quickly learn to lead our lives without looking at others and putting our house in order first, we are heading towards a social and mental breakdown as individuals. Fascinated with the concept of ***'whose role model are you?,*** I spent a long time speaking to scores of people on different aspects of leadership and inspiration. There were two things I learnt. First, it became clear that following a celebrity, be it a sportsperson or a movie star or a successful business is a very real affliction from which increasingly large numbers already suffer. It is the disease of compulsory adulation without which many feel life is meaningless. Second, I gradually got very appalled at how very little is known about actually being an inspiration rather than just being inspired by someone all the time. Earnest people talk bravely about 'being the change' or 'inspiring the young generation' but we know virtually nothing about how to do it.

This book is intended to do much more than present a theory. It also aims at demonstrating some steps to stop looking for role models and being one instead in 9 simple steps. And finally, and by no means less, this book sets out to change the reader in a subtle yet significant sense. For reasons that will become clear in the pages to follow, coping with inspiration in a measured way will require most of us to adopt a stance with a new awareness of the future. The degree to which the reader, after reading this book, finds himself thinking about, or speculating about, inspiring others will provide a true measure of its effectiveness.

Praise for the Book

"Will put high recommendation for this book for providing practical approaches towards interpreting & operating life. The novel shift is in the author's approach from modelling others to inculcate traits in self to become a model one self. A good read indeed. Examples too are quite relatable and the real life examples are truly gems to comprehend the concepts. The book is power packed with many real examples. Very insightful & truly inspiring."

—Shantanu Das Sharma

Best Selling Author - Awaken the Incredible Within

~~~

"This book will inspire people who are looking for motivation, mentoring and a growth guide. ***It's Time to Inspire*** is a guide for inspiring yourself. The book serves as a stepping stone to look within for motivation"

—Raj Singh

Best Selling Author - Digital the New Normal for Banks

~~~

"The book "It's Time to Inspire" is wonderfully articulated by Shridhar Aiyer, and provides you with a completely different perspective of how each one of us is leader but in fact, it's only our own mental blocks that makes us feel 'lesser' than what we really are. The book is an eye-opener, because while the general feeling is to be inspired by a role model, it makes you wonder *'how can I be a role model for others?'*. It also throws up several questions to ponder – *'What's my purpose in life that is driving me to perform? What creativity can I bring into my work that will be appreciated and followed by others?'*. I strongly recommend this book to anyone who wishes to change tracks and push themselves higher to become a leader, a role-model who can inspire others."

—Shyam Kalle

Best Selling Author – The Unbound Transformation

~~~

"In the times when world need more leaders than followers 'It's time to inspire' is like a light house that guides people towards acknowledging their gifts of innate leadership. The book not only talks about important traits of a leader but also presents a guide map for achieving the same. Anyone who would read this book will definitely achieve the higher level of personal and professional growth. My best wishes, may this lamp of knowledge light millions of houses."

—Poonam Negi

Best Selling Author – "Password of Abundance.
Unfolding the Secret of Life

~~~

"The way Shridhar has articulated the different aspects of leadership and inspiration is appreciated. Based on the concept of 'whose role model are you?' Shridhar has nicely demonstrated the same with ease which will make more sense to the reader. Great work indeed."

—Ashwini Kumar Raj,
Best Selling Author - My Life: Experiential Learning

~~~

"I highly recommend Shridhar's book which can help any sincere reader to get onto that journey of self discovery, and to get ready to inspire several fellow human beings. This book holds your hand through that journey of becoming a truly inspirational leader."

–Deepa Nagarajan
Best Selling Author - Women on Board
~~~

Contents

CHAPTER 1

Are You a Leader? Take Charge of Your Own Life First

Who am I?

I am a leader!

Before you start reading this book, I would like to share a truth that you might or might not be mindful of. 'We all have descended on this big blue marble to lead and not to be led.' Each one of us has the potential to invade the hearts and souls of others by our fantastic capabilities. It is in our DNA to become a life-changer to others. The great forces of nature like sun, moon and wind are committed to add radiance to each one of our lives but unfortunately, we chose to spend our whole life in a dark corner and keep ourselves far-flung from the leader within us. Astonishingly, there are only 1% people on this planet who have learnt to churn their capabilities into a head-turner personality and inspire others. Yes, there are only 1% of people who are actually successful and rest 99% are either average or below average. Factually, they are the ones who are the leaders and rest 99% are following them. 1:99! Is this not too much of unequal distribution?

Whenever we find ourselves fallen between the cracks, we look for external sources of motivation. We forget the fact that we are the sturdy rocks and a rock needs no protection from rain.

Let's look at the frog's Perspective

Once a group of frogs was merrily hopping through the forest. They did not have a care in the world until two of the frogs fell into a deep pit. All of the other frogs quickly gathered around the large pit and peered down into its deep vastness. They all began to scratch their heads trying to come up with a way to help. After a long period of time,when they couldn't think of a solution, they all agreed it was hopeless and yelled down to the two frogs to prepare for their fate and that they would never get out. Unwilling to believe the other frogs, the two frogs jumped even higher. The ones above the hole began to shout even louder to quit, to give up, that they would never get out of there alive and it wasn't worth it.

After a period of time, one of the frogs gave heed to what others were saying and gave up and died. However, the other frog jumped even higher. The shouts of discouragement continued and got louder. And though he was absolutely drained of every bit of energy he had, this determined frog continued to jump even higher – in miraculous ways. Eventually he jumped so high he sprang right out of the pit.

The other frogs celebrated this frog's victory and then gathered around him in puzzlement. They said, "Did you not hear us telling you to stay down, you wouldn't get out?" In response to that the frog said, "Oh, is that what you were saying? I am hard of hearing, and I thought you were telling me to jump higher. I didn't think you were discouraging me, I thought you were encouraging me."

Similarly, since childhood, we have been conditioned to follow others. When we were kids, our young ears were often instructed to follow our elder siblings and other brilliant classmates. "Look at your elder sister; she is better than you in studies, why don't you learn from her?"When we grow up, we are asked to idolize others. Often, we are asked to follow the ones whom we do not even know. In the Indian context we often hear "Look at your uncle's son; he is an engineer and earning a lot of money. Why don't you do the same?"

Further, when we step in the corporate world, our heads are often hammered with, "Follow your seniors and colleagues who are more efficient." Of course, there is no harm in learning from others but this way we unknowingly become a part of the herd race. We actually tend to overlook our own identity and do what others are doing. To put it in other words, 'the glorified lives of others impresses us more than even our own life'.

We usually hear stories about people from a humble background becoming the Prime Minister, President and the greatest entrepreneurs. However, such stories often inspire us for a few minutes or maybe days and later taking charge of our own lives becomes something extra-terrestrial to us. The truth is we have programmed ourselves in a way that we feel more comfortable being the follower rather than being a leader.

We forget the fact that 'once a follower, always a follower and once a leader **always** a leader.' We rely more on the external sources to motivate us and we turn a deaf ear to the statement that we have piles of motivation lying dormant in ourselves. All we need to do is, to give that snoozing leader a wakeup call and register our name in the list of the great leaders to have ever treaded on this earth.

What does it take to become a leader?

Now since we have ignited the determination to become a leader, first of all, let's learn about who actually a leader is. Well, leaders are the beacon of change; they are the lighthouse to others. Leaders are the unique people who are distinct because they think differently. They do not think like followers. Factually, 'all the leaders were followers at one time'. However, they pushed the paddle to the metal and evolved as great leaders.

If you want to be an impactful personality, you need to develop certain thinking patterns and perceptions that change the way you see yourself. Let's talk about 6 proven traits that can transform you into a life-changing leader:

Take the Lead; Take Charge of your Life

The first step to be become a leader is to **take charge of your life**. Let your life not be governed by others. Most of us are nothing more than aimless wanderers. Usually, it is others who are steering our life. If you want to cruise to the top of the pyramid, you need to stop hurling excuses and make it happen. Recently, I was in the middle of a coaching session for a corporate manager. During the conversation, he informed that his boss, who was a great leader, had resigned. He said that he would be missing his boss since he was a great combination of leadership and skills.

When he was done with the praise, I asked him, "So now are you going to handle his position?" The question made him spellbound for a few seconds. He smiled and said, "I am not that talented as he was. Maybe in few years I can think of applying for that position." We often underestimate ourselves, which restricts us from taking charge of our life. We, knowingly or unknowingly have convinced our upper head that we are born to be followers.

However, we are in a situation of 'now or never'. Most of us are stuck in the role of the victim, blaming everything and everyone but ourselves for what is and what is not happening for us. When we hand the control of our life to others, this is a likely outcome. If we continue being a puppet to other's and keep blaming our background, parents, teachers, bosses, the economy and the society for everything that's negative in our lives, nothing is going to change. You need to take control of the strings of your life.

Each day you have the ability for choosing to take control of your life, or to let it control you. You can either be proactive, or you can be reactive by allowing various circumstances or people to navigate you the way they want.

Vision

Leadership is all about seeing and creating a brighter and better future. It's about inventing, innovating, creating, building, improving, and transforming every aspect of our lives and the world we live in. Leaders have a clear vision about where they are going and what they are trying to accomplish. Some scoff when leaders share bold ideas, imaginative goals, and seemingly impossible dreams, but ideas, imagination, and dreams are the fabric that *positive* leaders weave together to create the future and change the world.

At one time, *Star Wars* was just an idea in the mind of George Lucas, but now the Force is as strong as ever. J.K. Rowling had a vision of Harry Potter and now he is an iconic part of our life—and as real as a roller-coaster in Universal Studios. John F. Kennedy had a vision for sending a man to the moon. Ronald Reagan saw the Berlin Wall come down before it crumbled. Steve Jobs imagined the iPod and iPhone long before the world was addicted to them. Abraham Lincoln envisioned a united America. Martin Luther King, Jr., had a dream about equality.

A positive leader sees what's possible and then takes the next steps to rally and unite people to create it. Every invention, project, creation, and transformation starts with an idea, an imagination, and a vision of what's possible. History evinces that if you can see it, you can create it. If you have a vision, then you also have the power to make it happen. Positive leaders tap into the power of a vision and find a way forward. But in order to inspire people to follow you, you must be able to articulate and communicate your vision in a simple, clear, bold, and compelling way.

Attitude

The next quality of an influential leader is attitude. Here attitude does not mean arrogance or over-confidence. A leader has the attitude that makes him/her different from the followers. We all know about the king of the jungle; the lion. Factually, the lion is not the tallest, largest, most intelligible or the heavy weight animal in the woods. Still, what makes him the king of the jungle? Attitude!

This evidences that to be the king, you do not need to be the most intelligent or muscled or prowl with any kind of advantage and yet you can be the leader. Therefore, the lion cancels all your excuses for not becoming a leader.

"I am not afraid of an army of lions let by a sheep, I am afraid of an army of sheep led by lions."

—Alexander the Great

'Attitude is altitude'. Leaders can transform cowards into warriors.Great leaders inspire other people, their friends, customer, associates and even their children because they are inspired themselves. They are excited about the possibility of creating an exciting future for themselves. They get up every morning and they see every effort they make as part of a great plan to accomplish something wonderful in their lives and push forward with a positive attitude. Great leaders see themselves as victors over circumstances rather than victims of circumstances. They do not criticize or blame others when things go wrong. Instead, they focus on the solution, on what can be done that can cruise them out of troubled waters.

Remember, 'it is you, only you, who can take charge of your attitude.'

Here are some ways that can help you engineer a leadership attitude:

- Build your self-esteem
- Take an exit from toxic associations; ignore whiners and complainers
- Create a library of 'positive' thoughts
- Avoid negative electronic input especially negative feeds on social media
- Brush up your vocabulary with more positive words

- Focus more on solutions rather than problems
- Be courteous while interacting with anyone around you

Belief System

If you want to live beyond what you are living today, you need to change your belief system. Leaders are born when they conspire the discovery of a new belief system. You might have the potential but if you do not have your belief system in place, success might keep repulsing from you. Your life is what you think it should be. What you are today, is what you thought to be. And if you do not like what you are today, you need to change your belief system. That is how leaders are born. Your leadership is determined by 3 factors:

1. The perception of who you are
2. The reason why you think you exist
3. Your sense of significance

Usually, we form perceptions based on what others think of us. Therefore, you must change these three perceptions; who you are, the reason what you think is behind your existence and your sense of significance. You are born to do something significant in this world. Here, let me share a story with you.

There was a boy who was from a poor family. He was slow in learning to speak. He was not able to compete with other kids of his age.One day, he came home and told his mother that he had been expelled from the school and the principal said that he would not be able to do much in life. His mother asked him not to worry and said, "Son, one day you would do big in life." She often fed the ears of the boy with 'you are good' assertion. After few years, his mother died. One day he while he was cleaning his house, he found a trunk gathering dust in the corner of the room. It was his mother's. He opened it and found a bundle of letters, which were written by his school principal. Every single letter said, 'your son is a dumb and he would be a loser in life'.

However, at that time, the letters were nothing more than an object of fun to him. Who was that boy? Albert Einstein! What transformed him into a master from a disaster? His belief system that his mother kept feeding by telling him that he was good. She actually made him believe that he was the best, which got registered in his mind. This is the power of belief system.

Self-Driven

Leaders do not wait for others to give marching orders and do bare minimum, without exceeding anyone's expectations. Leaders are self-driven. The ones with above traits are followers and not leaders, who spend their entire life in mediocrity. The leaders do not wait to reach to the managerial position to display their leadership skills. Irrespective of the role they are in, they always work on the wrongs; they improve by taking relevant actions, without anyone asking them.

A good leader is a self-starter and self-driven to achieve a higher level of outcome compared to his or her peers. Three people were laying the bricks side by side on a construction site. When they were asked, "What is your job?" the first person answered, "My job is to do what I am told to do for eight hours a day so I can get a check." The second person replied, "My job is to lay the bricks." The third person said, "My job is to build an amazing monument."

Which of these three people do you think would be the happiest, most productive and go the extra mile? Indeed, the third person, who understood that his job was far greater than just laying the bricks. He understood he was contributing to a purpose greater than his own efforts.

All of us are in search of a clear and driving purpose in our lives; we want to contribute to something bigger than ourselves. The world of work offers a great opportunity for people to connect with a purpose. The reality is that people care less about working for a company and much more about working for a compelling cause. Hence, their minds might be engaged, but their hearts will not be. Therefore, a compelling purpose is the reason to be excited about getting up and going to work every day. Well, this is thesixth component to become a great leader; enthusiasm

Enthusiasm

The best leaders are enthusiastic. They have the ability to inspire others to work towards a particular mission. The best leaders know that enthusiasm will inspire and move people to action. Every single cell of their body is infused with passion. Enthusiasm is a kin to greatness, it's the brother of happiness and father of optimism and this is what an ideal configuration of a leader is. The best part is that enthusiasm is contagious. If you are zealous, you will see it getting poured in people around you.

Therefore, if you are not enthusiastic throughout the day, it is time to give yourself a wakeup call. Be happy, be grateful, be enthusiastic for the life that you have, for every single opportunity and also for the challenges that come your way. If you are spirited, you can overcome any challenge and this will make you even stronger. Challenges in your life do not come to dispirit you but to make you realize your hidden potential.

So, the leader is waiting inside you to be ignited. All you need to do is to incorporate these 6 qualities and live the life of a leader. Do not depend on others to motivate you or to become your pathfinder. It is no one else but you who have the finesse to take charge of your own life. Unless you do not inspire yourself, you will not be able to shine the torch for others.

Let the world witness the fantastic leader inside you!

CHAPTER 2

Who is Responsible for Your Success?

I happen to meet our next generation quite often in the colleges around the country. It is fantastic talking to them and getting to know them better. But there are times when I really get puzzled. Why? Because what I see is that almost everyone sitting out there is carrying a baggage of the last 20 years. And that talks about their entire life.

A rich kid in the crowd is still the same who lives with his rich parents and in their rich house. He or she has not left that environment yet and believes that every action of his or her is somehow linked to that atmosphere. Same goes for the poor/average kids. Our upbringing is a dominant factor in our heads and we don't want to let go of it. If you think this is prevalent only in young kids, then you should discern the adults as well.

I have spoken with some quite successful people who are way in their forties, who still blame their parents for something or the other. I have also spoken with many people who are way in their fifties, not doing well at all, and are convinced that their parents and their upbringing or neighborhood are the only reason for them being where they are in their lives. They are nothing more than a spinning wheel stuck in mud.

If you are not happy with your life, it's time you take a little inventory of sorts of your life.

Whatever you are today is the result of all the choices you have taken in the last 20 years of your life. And down the line 20 years, you will be, well, a result of the choices you start taking from today. And what is the choice after all? A right or a left? East or the west? Both directions will give you consequences. And the only person responsible for the upshot is you.

The origin of the word location is from the Latin word locus. People with an internal locus of control are of the opinion that they and only they are responsible for life and its journey. The ones with an external locus blame everybody they can think of and get old very soon.

Think about it, passing a buck doesn't make sense; it can be too detrimental for you and your life. Once you start blaming the circumstances, environment or for that matter your upbringing for certain sequences of life, certainly, it shows how weak you are and how irresponsible you can be towards yourself. Maybe there are instances where few decisions didn't work in your favor. But that doesn't qualify the fact that others were responsible for your failure. In fact, complaining and blaming is a job of failures, and it has done nothing but caused damage to their thinking process and self-esteem.

Isn't it quite strange that we blame others when we fail but when we taste success, we scream out loud for self-praise and give all the credit to none but ourselves? One cannot succeed alone; it needs support system of the team, colleagues, well-wishers, mentors, etc. Whereas, I believe that failure can be attributed to only self because other forces cannot work in opposition. Somehow, somewhere our mismanagement and wrong decisions have has influenced the outcome.

As self-centered human beings, we generally do whatever we think is right for us, even if someone tries to bring us to the right; we doubt the person's intentions. That shows we can take control of our lives in whatever situations, right or wrong. And we should certainly stop pointing fingers towards others or for that matter any circumstances or environment.

You chose a path to walk if encountered by failure or success; disappointment or disgrace, the credit goes to you, not to your teammates, colleagues, relatives or any situation for that matter.

Here are some recommended actions that would navigate you to the horizon of success: -

Embrace What Comes Your Way

This is really an important aspect of your existence, the belief in yourself is an achievement and it aspires you to conquer the world. Certainly, you should know that whatever you do will have direct repercussions on your outcome, actually, you are the person to yearn your life. It is just like a potter carving a pot out of the mud. Same is the case with an individual. He or she does shape up life with own hands by the positive outlook, deeds, attitude, behavior, perception, and perseverance, despite unfavorable conditions, disruptions and difficulties.

Take Account of Your Actions

Many of us are just convinced that there are many other forces other than within, which influence destiny, particularly when faced with failures and disappointments. Is that true? How can we even think about it when we ourselves are in control of your deeds and doings? There are times when you lose the track, things don't work the way you expected, be it in personal or on professional front. However, this is the time when one should not lose focus, rather stand strong and take the charge to settle things in the right perspective. It is only by your sincere efforts, you can hit back to the unwanted situation. Usually failures are a part of your miscalculations or misinterpretations, which are equally important at times to lead you to the road with a golden pavement. It would be very awful if you attribute them to the environment or upbringing or your surroundings. As they say, "a man learns by his mistakes".

Yes, better to take account of your doings. One who does so, will indeed emerge as a winner.

Be in a Complete Awe of Yourself

Your existence is a belief that you are here to achieve something great and to do that you have found ways within. There will be a support system to guide you, to provide you a shoulder to lay on, but finally, it is you who has to chalk out the way to success. And that path of success has never been a bed of roses to anybody for that matter. Way to success will come along its own bumps and thorns, challenges and hindrances. One has to be mentally and physically ready to overcome whatever comes in between you and success. Even if you encounter a failure, you should take it positively and gain an experience out of that.

Nothing is Impossible

The day when you will realize your potential and hidden treasures within, you will undoubtedly forge new reasons to accomplish the unaccomplished. Taking the full control and responsibility of your life and goals, including your failures, not so pleasant moments, unwanted results and objectives is the only way to survive and surcharge. When you will embrace your unhappiness happily, your failures successfully, your bad times in a good way, your downs with ups, that is the day when you will feel empowered and in charge of your destiny, followed by success.

If you peep into history, you will find that all successful people around the world have had an unwavering belief in themselves, be it good or bad. They made mistakes, rather blunders, they tasted bitterness, they felt pain and agony, just to taste that sweetness of success in the bigger picture. Successful people have inspired us through their risk-taking ability to achieve the impossible, but if you understand their philosophy, it reveals that they have chosen thorns over roses, they have chosen bumpy roads over the smooth rides, they have chosen so to create their own success story and not engage in a blame game, holding the circumstances accountable. Successful people create a niche for themselves only after taking challenges and impossible tasks to prove their caliber to none but themselves.

For example - We all know the success story of Cristiano Ronaldo, but do you know there are many hardships he faced, like, his family's financial condition was not that great, still, he followed his passion, his parents were not highly literate, he was expelled from the school. But he still persisted his goal and now he is here to go nowhere.

It may sound strange, but believe that you have the power to change or topple failure into success. By learning from your mistakes, by being optimistic about the barriers you come across, you will be able to bolster your confidence to drift towards success.

Introspect and Inspect

Look within and inspect what is wrong and what can be set right? Who is wrong and who will undo it. You will find answers and solace. Most likely, all the answers lie within you because it is only you who will make a difference to YOU. If you are feeling like giving up in difficult situations, if you are feeling lazy to overcome stress, if you are feeling tired to get going, it is you, who has to get charged and push yourself to set things right. Because the fact is, these all problems are related to you and you should know the cure. It is all about YOU, not someone else.

Let me tell you a story of long ago. I was in a boarding school, it was exam time and one night I fell sick and the following day was the Math exam. My body was aching; I almost gave up and slept till dawn. When I reached the exam hall and received my question paper, I was blank. I had no clue, no formulas remembered. Even my friends with whom I shared my room, things and eatables were of no help in the exam hall. My teachers, who used to appreciate my sincerity towards subject, were strict to their duty. It was like a doom's day, where only you and you will be punished for your deeds. I was totally dismayed with the situation. There was no escapism, so I decided to take hold and gather strength and shook my mind to solve few sums for the sake to get at least minimum qualifying. Finally, on result day I could feel the sense of achievement and took pride that it was me just me who had passed the subject though I barely passed. Contrarily, had I surrendered, it was me who had failed and invited the wrath of my teachers and parents. Thence, there are times when situations are not in favor, you need to introspect and find out ways to turn the situation in your favor.

Life is like that exam hall where no friendship, no faltering, no angelic support or parental support comes to rescue. You only have to make efforts to come out successful even from the face of failure. Whatever the result, it is by you, for you, of you. We cannot evade the responsibility of our life and destiny, and it is foolish to put blame on others. It is you who has to make things desirable for yourself, to make sad things happy, to change the pain into a smile, to change the ifs and buts into 'yes I can'. You have to make extra efforts and make a firm mind to set things right for you.

Go Get Up and Set It

If you keep this motto of your life, I am very firm that you will never complain of others being responsible for whatever the situation. Because you will be convinced that it is ME, who has to take action, others are forces and they are there to guide me not ride my destiny.

Change is Inevitable

Nothing remains constant; if you feel like current strategies and plans are not working for you, change them. 'Same actions will fetch same results. You need to act differently to magnetize different results.' If you feel that something is going wrong and not the way you had thought, change the way you were doing it. Change your outlook for the world and the people around you. If the results excepted are not desirable, change the process. Though there is a lot of speculation, you will find resistance to change, but then there is no choice other than accepting it. Complaining and blaming will take you nowhere; instead it will cut on your time, energy and efforts.

Success is not a One-time Affair

Consistency, persistence, and perseverance play a huge role in what you are. The choice is yours, whatever you want to do with your life, either do it or leave it. The onus lies with you. Way to success is full of humps, how you overcome them is your liability. Indeed, you take support and suggestions from people who have been successful to reach to the other side of the road, but then it is you who has to walk on it with utmost endurance and persistence. Achievements and aspirations have a different meaning for different people, what worked for them may not work for you. Hence, you have to choose your way with your outlook and behavior. Your perception towards life and success may be different, while as other's may be entirely opposite. Yes, each individual has his or her own perspective of looking at things. You will have to lead your life towards success by looking at things in your perspective, not expecting others to look in the same manner. One good step will help you take better steps and gradually you will achieve your success.

Take Credit

Look back and feel good, the way we usually blame God or luck for our failure. Instead, credit yourself for success; take pride in getting success by your sincere and persistent efforts. The success story belongs to you as you are the main character in the script of your life. Whatever you chose to do, just take full control.

Thinking is Must

Don't worry, nothing is impossible in this world, but thinking makes it so. You need to adhere to the fact that none other than you is responsible for your life. It might seem a bit painful as well. But this pain is just to boost your worth. Each step taken will add to your journey when you lead your own road, rest will follow the suit.

Empower Yourself

It will improve your self-esteem and self-belief rather than waiting for someone to give you directions and guidance. It is far way beneficial to self-praise yourself with the affirmation,'I can do it' (we will learn more about affirmations in a chapter to follow). Empowering yourself will increase your worth and would capacitate you to take decisions, especially in the tough times.

Accept Yourself

Love the way you are, accept your faults with dignity, take a pride in making some good decisions. It will build your confidence in your abilities and also help to identify your mistakes. It elevates your self-perception to the extent that you feel accomplished.

Keep Low on Expectations

This is highly dangerous to keep expectations from others. It is to doubt your capabilities and makes you unable to take decisions for yourself, to take the lead. It stops your growth and ability to think beyond.

Self-praise

Don't wait for others to give a pat for your good work; people are miser in doing that. Take stock of your talent and appreciate yourself for good work. It will give you a sense of achievement and will boost your morale.

We are fully responsible for our success or failure. There are forces to guide us, help us, support us, but finally, we have to write our own destiny. As you sow, so shall you reap. You, yourself are your promoter, marketer, and designer of your life. It depends on how you control your life to reach your goals. I learned a lot from my failure and am still learning.

When we even go for an interview, it all depends on how we fair on the interview table. Either we get rejected or selected. Only we are responsible, few people blame the mood, ambiance, luck and what not. Those are just lame excuses to fail.

One should be convinced of the fact that, that there can be imperfections in life, but we should not buy negative conclusions and feel that they are good for nothing. It will further deteriorate your confidence and will make you more incapable. It is imperative to know that only you alone can rectify the damage. It is a human tendency that, they are most of the time in denial mode, you are mature enough to take over yourself and your success. You ought to take charge of your life, your emotional state.

Your actions, attitude and aptitude make you what you want to be, which proves that only you stay accountable for your life. You are likely to be successful if you stand by the fact that, 'I am responsible for my success'. But if you hold liable other circumstances like parents, luck, uncontrollable elements, then you are doomed to fail.

Go tell your story and let the world know, who is responsible for your success!

CHAPTER 3

Plan for Future; Live for Today

Planning

Once there lived a princess who was sent to a far off land by her father to study. However, when the princess came back, she was stunned; the wicked viceroy had killed her father and declared himself king. The shocked princess fled to the jungle. After wondering around for more than a week in the woods, the starved princess came upon a small hut. As she tried to approach the hut with her trembling feet, she fainted at the door. When she awoke, she found herself in a hermit's hut. She narrated her story to the hermit.

Hermit: "You have suffered grievously. What do you propose to do?"

Princess: "Sir, I am helpless! Please help me regain my kingdom."

Hermit: "Arise! I will help you. We need to formulate a plan."

Princess: "Plan?"

Hermit: "Yes, plan. Don't you want to punish the viceroy and get back your kingdom?

Thus began the princess's training. On the first day the hermit asked her some questions.

"Where are we presently?"

Princess: "In the forest."

Hermit: "Where do you want to be?"

Princess: "In my kingdom; ruling over it."

Hermit: "How do you PLAN to repossess?"

The princess was silent. The hermit smiled and said, "This is where you learn about planning."

What is a Plan?

Planning is a process for accomplishing the purpose. It is a blueprint of the map to success. It helps in deciding objectives; both in quantitative and qualitative terms. It is about deciding in advance; **what to do** and **how to do**. Planning bridges the gap between where we are to where we intend to go. It makes possible things to occur, which would not otherwise occur.

What Should a Plan be?

A plan should be a realistic view of the expectations. Depending upon the activities, a plan can be short-ranged or long-ranged or in other words; short-term and long-term plans. It is a framework within which it must operate.

Preparation of a comprehensive plan might not guarantee success but lack of a sound plan would almost certainly ensure failure.

Planning can be summarized in 3 easy steps:

1. Choosing a destination,
2. Evaluating alternative routes and
3. Deciding the specific cause of your plan.

Why is it Important to have a Plan?

It is important to prepare a plan keeping in view the goal you are aiming at. A plan is an important aspect to gain triumph over any goal. It serves the following 3 critical functions:

1. It helps in managing yourself,
2. It provides a logical framework within which you can structure strategies and
3. It offers a benchmark against which you can measure your actual performance and review it.

Hermit: "For instance, you have the choice to either capture your kingdom or live in exile. Since you have decided to capture your kingdom, you can decide amongst various alternatives on how to go about it.

Choice 1: You can claim the help of other kings who are your sympathizers.

Choice 2: Your erstwhile subjects can help you.

Princess: "Sir, why is planning so important?"

Hermit: "The ancients have always said, "The journey of a thousand miles begins with one step. Create a definite plan for carrying out your desire and begin at once whether you are ready or not to put this plan into action."

This very simple quote encapsulates the importance of planning. It helps in bridging the gap between the present and future course of action.

Benefits of Planning

- Planning reduces uncertainty, risk and confusion in operation. Through planning, the course of action is known to all and so you know what exactly needs to be done.
- Planning empowers your decision-making ability and full-proofs your action plan.
- Planning helps in identifying deviations and taking the corrective actions.
- Planning with an element of flexibility makes you more capable of coping with the changing environment and taking challenges head-on.
- It capacitates you to handpick best methods out of available choices, thus, reducing overlapping and wasteful activities.

- Planning helps you to review the progress periodically and recast the strategies to meet the objectives.

Hermit: "Remember you are born to win but to be a winner, you must plan to win, prepare to win and expect to win."

Princess: "Sir, will this help me win back my lost kingdom?"

Hermit: "Why not? Principles are meant to be applied in real life. A Plan is a blue-print of how you execute your dream in real life. Plans are nothing; planning is everything."

With this enlightened knowledge, the princess made her plans. Her subjects were loyal to her and ultimately she dethroned and imprisoned the wicked viceroy. The princess ruled over her kingdom wisely and well.

And what about the hermit? Well, he became her Prime Minister and used all his skills to guide the princess to maintain peace and prosperity.

"The more you sweat in practice,
the less you bleed in war."

—Richard Marcinko, Rogue Warrior

So friends, this is the power of planning. It can transform unachievable into obtainable. A structured plan can benefit not just you but also people around you. Investor Warren Buffett says, *"Someone's sitting in the shade today because someone planted a tree a long time ago."* Make sure you have a shady tree in your own future by planning for it in the present.

Mindset

After you have planned, you need to execute the plan but before that you need to fuel something; your **MIND**. You need to prepare your mindset to transmute your plan into action. When it comes to mindset, people believe that their basic qualities like talent or intelligence are inborn and cannot be changed. Authentically, 'they are wrong'. The good news is that you have a choice to change your mindset. Mindsets are just beliefs that we form about us, others and situations. It is our mindset that shapes our life, the actions we take and the possibility of magnetizing success or failure in future.

How important is your mindset?

The growth mindset (the belief that you are in control of your own ability, and can learn and improve) is the key to success. Of course, hard work, effort, and persistence are all significant, but not as vital as fostering the underlying belief that you are in control of your own destiny.

Your mindset will determine if you would be remembered or forgotten. Your mindset will determine whether you will be committed to cruise out of the trouble waters. Yes, it is your mindset that will determine if you will be a ***follower or a leader***. No human goes through life without challenges. Remember, 'when the going gets tough, the tough gets going'. Your mindset is indisputably your greatest asset.

Fixed VS Growth Mindset

According to work by pioneering Stanford psychologist Carol Dweck and others, the best predictor of success in life is none of these usual suspects-it's your mindset. Those who achieve great things generally believe they can improve and grow as people. This is called asthe "growth mindset." Those who are frustrated in their attempts to realize their dreams tend to believe their abilities and talents are static, a.k.a. they have a "fixed mindset." Let's understand the difference between the two with an example:

The ***fixed mindset*** says, "Are you sure you can do it? Maybe you don't have the talent."

The ***growth mindset*** answers, "I'm not sure I can do it now, but I think I can learn to with time and effort."

Fixed mindset: "What if you fail- you'll be a failure?"

Growth mindset: "Most successful people had failures along the way."

History is the proof that the world's greatest achievers have proved their mettle by going against the current, when the situations were completely unfavorable. How? By working on their growth mindsets! Friends, challenges and unfavorable situations are a part of life. "There is nothing called as failure, either you succeed or you learn."

If your mindset says, "I will do whatever it takes", you can transmute failures into stepping stones.

"I have not failed; I have just found 10,000 ways that won't work."

—Thomas Edison

What is Positive Thinking?

Our ears are often instructed with the statement, "Do not be a negative thinker. Be positive". However, it sounds like easier said than done. Most of us often find ourselves tangled in negative mindset and we keep drifting towards oceanic desolation despite Herculean efforts. We are often worried more about the failure than the happiness that would transpire upon success. Negative thoughts, words and attitude, breed negative and dejected feelings, mental-state and hence, behavior. When the mind is set on a negative mode, poisons are released into the blood, which mushroom unhappiness and negativity. These are what eventuate in failure, frustration and disappointment.

However, "positive thinking is not about expecting the best to happen every time but it is about accepting that whatever happens is the best for this moment." We often say that my life is like an uphill battle, there are so many problems in my life. When we harbor such negative statements in our mind, it leaks our energy. Researches have proved that negative words or statements not only make our mindset toxic but also our body and wellbeing.

Whereas, positive words infuse our mind and body with confidence. Contrarily, we can reiterate the same statement in a different way by saying, "There are many learning opportunities in my life."

"It's not the mountain that we climb that wears us out; it's the pebble in our shoe."

—Mohammad Ali

Similarly, negative mindset is what retards our speed and drifts us away from accomplishments. However, if we replace it with positive mindset, we come across more opportunities to make our way to the throne of leadership.

Here are 9 significant steps that can help you spruce your growth mindset:

1. Believe in yourself
2. Take challenging situations head-on
3. Take failures as stepping stones
4. Surround yourself with leaders and not followers
5. Journalize the skills that can gain you fistful of confidence
6. Say a big 'NO' to procrastination
7. Take learning as an ever-ending process
8. Always be open to feedbacks
9. Don't be reluctant to find a mentor

Now, that you have groomed your mindset, it's time to bungee jump and get into action mode.

Action

This is the area where most of us fail to carry out and hence we tend to blame our destiny, people and even situations. Besides, this is what demarcates the line between a leader and a follower or observer. We spend a great deal of time while planning and building our mindset, but when it comes to action, we often take a back seat due to some kind of fear or doubt. We again resolve to fall into the 'learning traps'.

Now, here's a simple math question for you:

5 frogs are sitting on a log.

4 of the frogs decide to jump off. How many frogs are left?

Did you answer 1?

The correct answer is still 5. This is because there is a difference between deciding and doing.

Have you experienced this in your own life? We tend to make a lot of decisions. We decide to eat healthier, double our income in next two years, buy a house in next five years or start a new business. However, all of the planning and mindset combing goes down the drain when not alloyed with appropriate actions.

Planning and mindset building are although crucial but these are just the preliminary preparations. These are like equipping yourself with the life jacket and headgear. But to reach the destination, you need to cut through the waters and flap your way to the blissful horizon. Yet most people seldom transport themselves from the planning to action mode. By getting into the habit of putting ideas and decisions into action, we are in a better position to achieve the results we desire.

"Your beliefs become your thoughts; your thoughts become your words; your words become your actions; your actions become your habits; your habits become your values; your values become your destiny."

—Anonymous

Rather people prefer to procrastinate by sitting beside the gushing stream and waiting for the tides to calm down. Procrastination is the number one reason why most people never get to accomplish their goals and reach their dreams.

Here are 6 proven ways to transport you from deciding into action mode:

1. Stop waiting until conditions are perfect

If you are waiting for things to get in your favor to get started, you will be waiting forever. Things will never be perfect. There will always be something that would be unfavorable or could be even better. There is no right time; there is only the present time. This is the right time to take action and you can always be flexible as you move along.

"The best time to plant a tree was 20 years ago. The second best time is now."

—Chinese Proverb

2. "No matter how you feel, get up, dress up and show up." —Regina Brett

Restyle yourself into a doer. A doer is someone who has a plan and balanced mind and moves forward with it immediately. Have you ever asked your friend, "It's raining outside, let's go for a cup of coffee," and then rather spend time dozing off in bed? Next time,'get up, dress up and show up'. Do you often decide to go for a morning walk or to the gym and often end up hitting the snooze button? Now is time to abolish the slothful approach and dive in action mode. When we pause and wait, we lose the will to move forward and allow the doubtsand lame excuses to sneak into our minds.

3. Stop over-assessing

When we over-analyze things, we confine ourselves in the paralysis of analysis. We start to dissect things so deeply that it immobilizes us. For instance, you are driving from one city to another, which is at a distance of about 100 kilometers. While you have just crossed 10 kilometers, you come across an unfortunate accident. Now, if you start analyzing the cause behind the accident, if there were any causalities and start imagining if that could have happened with you, do you think you would be able to reach safe to your destination safe? May everyone reach to one's destination safe and sound but in this case; there could be a chance that you might hit someone while being overcautious.

4. Take continuous action

Once you get started, make continuous action your regime. Make sure that you move one step closer to your dream by doing something productive related to your idea every day or on a regular basis. This can be as easy as assigning, let's say, 15 minutes, completing a small task daily. Those small tasks will contribute significantly and help you gain confidence by witnessing achievement.

"Small Strokes fell great oaks."

—Benjamin Franklin

You just need this schedule into a habit. We are creatures of habits. Successful people are successful because they travel one mile extra than others. And hence, they take more action because they have made it their habit.

Professional athletes like Tiger Woods, Michael Jordan, Cristiano Ronaldo, Lionel Messi, Lin Dan, etc., **they all turned practice into their habits** while other ordinary players find it difficult to practice every day.

5. Use your action to overcome fear

Fear of failure is what pulls us back most of the times. Do you know that is the most fearful thing in the list of World's Top 10 Fearful things? It is not the snake or crocodile or a tiger. It is 'public speaking'. Most people experience trembling in their legs when they are asked to address an audience. Even the most experienced and poised speakers can get highly strung during this time. However, do you know the most tragic part? Everyone wants to be heard!

However, once you start taking appropriate actions, like mirror practice, mock practice, addressing friends, etc., this fear will start to take an exit route. In my opinion, if this world's most dreaded fear can be shooed away by actions, then any other fear can. So, action and only action can be a cure for fear. If you find yourself shaky or distressed, get into the action mode and you would be shocked by the upsurge of confidence.

6. Ward off the Distractions

How many times does it happen that one day you wake up and you resolute to finish all the pendency at your office desk? You not only decide to clear the pending work but also take some extra work to impress your boss. But the time you reach your desk while being pumped with confidence, you get distracted by the Whatsapp or Facebook message notification beep on your phone. Or probably, you think of having a cup of coffee with your colleague. We live in a world of tempting distractions. Such intrusions can prevent us from being productive and give us an excuse to procrastinate. This is what most of the dreamers do and this is what most of the leaders ward off.

The simple truth is that one average idea put into action is far more valuable than 20 genius ideas that are being saved in the pipeline for some other day or the right time. When you have an idea or made a decision, get into the habit of taking action. Jump off the log and discover all of the amazing things you can accomplish.

It is alright if you delay your actions and put them off once in a while. However, you have to understand that if your procrastination has become a habit, it will be very dangerous for you.

Therefore, it is always advisable to prevent it and get rid of procrastination before it becomes permanent in you and destroy your life.

Short-term and Long-term Goals

Let's begin with a simple question; what is a goal? Goals are a clear picture of where you want to be. It is about what your life would be if you succeed in embarking those changes. Absence of goals would be like running a marathon that has no finish line. In this case, even if you are able to achieve something, it would not feel like an achievement. Therefore, by the end of this chapter, you will be able to draw finish lines in your life.

If you notice the sailors, they have a compass with them all the time. Why do they carry that compass? So that they can navigate to their destination without getting lost in the tides of the colossal sea. Similarly, we all need a direction; we ought to have a purpose so that we do not get lost in our lives. Therefore, goal setting is quite crucial for all of us. Both short-term and long-term goals motivate us to be focused and productive. However, it is important to know the difference between the two.

Short-Term Goals

As the name suggests, short-term goals are those goals that have a short timeline, which could be of today, a week, a month or a year. Some examples of short-term goals could be buying grocery while on the way back home, or taking family for outing on the weekend, or paying the annual insurance premium.

Therefore, we need to have well-set short-term goals in order to accomplish our long-term goals. We must be cognizant of what we want from our life and to get that, we should have a well-organized daily plan. Let's say, you want to learn driving. You cannot learn the nuts and bolts or driving in one day. You need to understand the mechanics of how a car operates. In addition, you also need to gain some knowledge on some technical aspects like the checking the battery water or oil level or how to replace a punctured tyre. You need to go step-by-step or in other words, mile-by-mile. Eventually, after a few weeks or months of efforts, you would gain confidence of driving on busy streets.

Long-Term Goals

Long-term goal is something you aspire to do in future. They are not something that you can do in this week or even this year. Long-term goals generally have a timeline of 12 months or more. At the same time, they include the completion of short-term goals. Here are some examples of long-term goals; graduating from college, saving for retirement, starting your own business, buying a house or property, etc.

Goals-Setting that could Transform your Life

If you have got big plans in life but no plan in place to work on, chances are that you are not going to reach to the desired destination. While addressing a seminar, I was asked by an attendee,"How to set goals that are clear, compelling and most importantly; that produce meaningful change?" Let's walk through the SMART procedure of setting goals that could prove to be a life-changer for you.

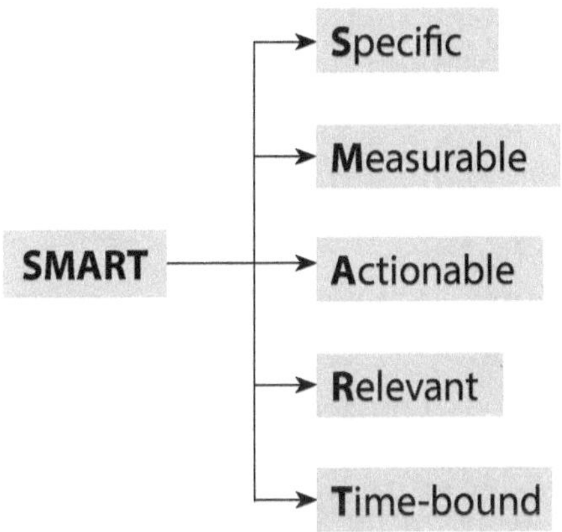

1. Specific

One should be specific while setting goals. I have come across people who say that they would buy a big house one day or they will think of losing weight from next month or that they would buy a sedan in next five years or one day they would get their dream job. In this case, the chances are rare that they would ever be able to lay hands on their desires. Why? Because even they are not clear of what exactly they want. They have a vague picture of their goals. I always suggest them to be specific by clearly defining their goal.

For instance, if one aspires to buy a sedan, in this case, one should be aware of the model, color, specifications and price of the car. It is only then that you start to send directions to your brain to start working on your dream. In this case, I even suggest the attendees to take a printout of their dream car and paste it on their office or bedroom wall. You may set the picture of that car as the desktop wallpaper on your computer or phone.

Similarly, saying that you want to be healthier, would take you nowhere. Rather, you should set a goal of replacing cold drinks with plain water, spending few minutes in gym every day. You can be even more specific, you may aim to drink one glass of water every two hours or you can say that every morning you would spend about an hour in the gym. Therefore, make it as specific as possible so you know what exactly you are going to be focusing on. This way, your mind gets a specific direction to work in, rather than just shooting in the dark and leaving it on destiny.

2. Measurable

Always set goals that are measurable so that you can gauge your progress and stay motivated, be it related to your work, learning or personal development. Tracking the progress of your goal is an important trigger to keep yourself motivated. It allows you to set milestones that you can celebrate when you achieve them and revaluate when you don't.

Avoid setting big plans which might result in falling flat and losing interest in working on the laid plan. For instance, you have set a goal to buy a house. This plan needs to be split in smaller plans or short-term goals. You may evaluate the investment that you need to buy the house and then you need to create a different savings account or wallet to fuel your dream. You may name it as; Dream-Home Account. You can divide that amount into number of monthly payments, which you will be depositing in your dream-home account. Now, every month you will be depositing the desired amount. Let's say, after 6 months, when you check the account balance, it would boost your confidence that you are on the way to fulfill your dream of your own or bigger house.

3. Achievable

Goals should be blueprinted like a good workout. They should make you push your limits slightly, so you feel challenged, but they should not impact you largely to cause some kind of stress or injury. For instance, you are earning 50,000 a month; you cannot set the target of taking your family on the world-tour in next six months. A poorly defined goal might find its place in trash after some time. Most of the people build a trap for themselves by setting unattainable goals. Therefore, instead of setting impossible goals, your goals should be challenging, yet achievable.

There is nothing wrong is shooting for the stars as you might end up on the moon. However, it is recommended to take small steps. For example, making one million by the end of the month is nearly impossible if you can't even pay your bills unless you have won a lottery. Therefore, an achievable goal would to make some extra thousand by the end of the month. Once you have achieved that, you can go one step further.

4. Relevant

A common issue that most of the people face is having too many goals at the same time or pursuing the wrong goal. I came across a client who spent three months learning guitar only to later realize that it was not what he wanted to learn. According to him, playing guitar would often keep him backstage and he wanted to remain in the front. Therefore, he decided to learn the vocals. Getting his fingers on the right string and right fret was impressive for him but it was not relevant to his overall life plan. It is just like, reaching to the top of the hill but still lacking enthusiasm to celebrate the victory.

Hence, ask yourself, 'why you want to achieve that goal', would the achievement really transport you to cloud nine?' If the answer comes back as 'No', withdraw yourself from the goal and try scribbling something that makes you lift your tight fisted hands in air and say "Yes, I have done it.' If the answer comes as 'Maybe', then you should rethink until you get clarity. If the answer comes as big 'YESSSS', then it is the right time to start chasing your goal.

5. Time-bound

This is one of the most important factors. Your plans must have a deadline. If you don't set a time limit, it would tell your brain that you have unlimited time to achieve your goals and hence the time would come when you would side-step that goal. However, when you are working on a deadline, your sense of urgency increases and you are more likely to achieve your goal.

Think of your time in school, during the summer vacations, you had two months to complete your holiday homework. However, usually you ended up completing the entire homework in last few days or week. It was only when the deadline was around the corner; we had no choice but to do it. Therefore, whenever you set a goal, keep a time limit in mind since it will push you to actually work on it.

Now that you know about setting SMART goals, there is one more thing that people usually miss on. People think that it is a one-time affair; they set their goals and after some days forget them. However, it is actually an ongoing process. Your plans will always need evaluation and revisions. There could be times when would notice that certain approach is not working. During such times, you need to be flexible by thinking of an alternate route to reach your goal. This is one of the major driving forces that differentiate between a follower and a leader. Followers are the ones who do what everyone else is doing, whereas the leaders set their own rules.

"Arise, awake and stop not till the goal is achieved."

—Swami Vivekanand

CHAPTER 4

Discipline and Hard Work: The only Key to Success

Discipline: The One Word that Makes a Difference

Let us first or all understand what discipline is. None of us can afford to live a life that is controlled by someone else. Hence, discipline means saying 'yes' to one and saying 'no' to the other 99, that are distractors. Discipline does not mean handcuffing yourself. It is about doing something that you had thought you would do, no matter what comes your way. Your mind would throw ample of distractions but you need to duck out the distractions and focus on your commitment. Another term for discipline is 'not listening to your mind' because the mind is fickle my friend. Your mind might not be able to stay on one thought for a long period of time and hence starts to catapult distracting excuses.

There was a client who approached me saying that had been working on the same level for 5 years and promotion was something that was miles away from him. Upon counseling, I came to know that he was although a sincere employee but his habit of saying 'yes' to everyone was the major reason behind him pushing is promotion away. Every time someone would approach him saying, "Hey Joe, I have a lot of work on my desk, would you mind sharing some of my work?", he would never say no even if he had more pending files sitting on his desk.

He worked for extended hours completing his and other's work while still left with a stack of pending files at his desk by the end of the day. Although he worked like a donkey but still he could not get the lion's share that he deserved. His boss would often warn him for leaving incomplete files on his desk to gather dust. Gradually, he was considered as incompetent since he was unable to complete his work on time, while others were, by transferring their spill over to him.

Therefore, the first thing I ingrained in him was to say 'no' while treating him with the tailored module. He called me after three months and said that his colleagues and boss were surprised by his changed approach. He in a jovial tone said that he had one more news to share, which was, he was shortlisted for the promotion interview, which had happened for the first time in five years.

Well, even I was delighted to know about the aftermath of his training sessions. I come across many clients who have had suffered in their lives because they are not able to ward off the distractions or temptations. Compromising with discipline can lead you to uninvited situations. Therefore, you should be committed to stay disciplined.

It is the discipline to stay committed not when everyone is watching but when no one is watching. It is the discipline to eat healthy foods when you have other tempting options. It is the discipline to choose to work hard when you have many escape routes available at your disposal. It is the discipline to get out of bed and jump in your tracksuit even if it is too hot or too cold outside. It is the discipline to keep going when the going gets tough because life does not give you what you want; it gives you what you deserve.

Remain faithful to yourself and your vision. Once, a reporter asked the all-time great boxer Mohammad Ali about the secret behind his elephantine strength. Ali replied, "10 pushups." The reporter giggled and asked, "Just 10 pushups?" To this the man with the golden glove replied, "No, 10 pushups after I am completely exhausted and about to fall on my knees!" This is what we call as the discipline to stay committed to one self.

There could be times even in the face of disciplined approach, what you might come across is failures one after another. This is where most of the people abolish the line of discipline and prefer stepping in the comfort zone. However, discipline is to keep trying. Everyday. Simple!

If I have to sum up the difference between the successful and average, the difference between the leaders and followers, there is only one word: ***Discipline***.

Remain disciplined and stay strong!

Hard Work

Let me be honest with you here. Friends, 'there are no shortcuts to success'. The only way to be successful is by pushing the pedal to the metal. 'Hard work is smart work', provided, it is in the right direction.We all wish to break-free from the clutches of ordinary and reach to the pinnacle. There are some people who desire a life that involves less of hard work and more of bliss. Among those, there are some people who are able to trek to the peak of the hill but still they feel something missing in life. What is that missing element that still makes them long for something that even they might not be cognizant of? It is the hard work that is missing in their life.

"If you want to shine like a sun, first burn like a sun."

—Dr. A.P.J. Abdul Kalam

Even the king of the jungle has to run at its top speed to earn its meal or it might starve to death. Similarly, it is the route of hard work that can tread you to success and not by merely charting route plans. It is your hard work that can help you attain new heights. Wait, this is not the end of the story. Even after reaching to the zenith, you need to continue with your meticulous work to stay at the same level. This statement might sound like a tough-grind to some. Well, trust me, worry won't help either. The best possible way to make your hard work as easy as a pie is to enjoy working hard. Make it a passion of your life. By brewing in the 'fun element', it won't look like a mountainous hard work anymore. 'Do what you love and love what you do.'

Talent VS Hardwork

Often people debate over if talent is more important or hard work. We all might have heard of the hare and tortoise story that our young ears were often fed with during the school days. If we try to assert a moral of the story in this context, what could it be? It's simple; there is no substitute for hard work. Talent can give a head-start but it is hard work that wins you applauses.

In fact, people who have been successful in life have understood the importance of hard work. They started their journey with some amount of talent but poured in a lot of hard work. This is what transpired their success with bells and whistles. Some may have more talent than other, however, what is that, that ensures a talented person wins; hard work.

We might have also heard of the story of King Bruce and the Spider. Bruce was a brave king. Once, he had to fight against a large army with just a few soldiers. After a long battle, he got defeatedand he had to run for his life. Bruce took shelter in a forest cave. He was very depressed. His courage had left him. He was blankly gazing at the ceiling of the cave when an interesting scene captured his attention.

A small spider was trying to weave a web across the cave ceiling. As the spider crawled up, a thread of the web broke and the spider fell down. But the spider did not give up. He tried to climb again and again. Finally, the spider successfully climbed up and completed the web.

Bruce began to think, "If a small spider can treat failure with hard work, why should I give up? I will try with all might till I win". This thought gave strength to the defeated king.

Bruce got out of the jungle and collected his brave soldiers. He fought against the large army. He was defeated again. But now, he would not give up his fight. Bruce again and again fought against the large army and finally, after many attempts, defeated the large army and regained his kingdom. He had learnt a lesson from the spider. 'Never give up.'

Consistent hard work is the key to succeed. Similarly, it took Colonel Saunders 69 attempts to bake the Kentucky Fried Chicken that is world renowned today. Therefore, we should not give up and be consistent in our efforts. Hard work is something that is in our hand, that we can utilize as a tool to achieve our goals. It can covert pebbles into diamond because diamond in a raw form is nothing more than a stone. It is the polishing that makes it a diamond.

Let me share an interesting story with you, which showcases the ideal combination of discipline and hard work. There was a couple in Argentina. The man was a factory worker and the woman was a part-time cleaner. They led their life as a lower-middle class couple. Then came the day when they became parents, the woman gave birth to a boy. Unfortunately, the son was born with a hormone deficiency disorder. He could not grow as fast the kids of his age. The boy grew up with a short stature but he enjoyed playing football. However, because of his short height, no football team would take him as their team member because you need a certain type of built to play any sport. Nevertheless, he did not lose hope.

One day, he asked his parents, "Can you not get me treated? Can we not consult a doctor? Why can I not become normal?" So his parents took him to a doctor and then to a specialist, then to another specialist and so on. The parents were informed that it would cost them $900/ month to get their son treated. The poor parents could barely afford the household expenses and did not have that much money to take care of their kid's treatment. His father told him about the expenses involved and told his son in a heavy voice that he would not be able to get him treated. The son replied, "It is ok father. I still want to play. They may not take me in the team but they cannot stop me from playing."

This kid kept playing day in and day out. Eventually, he was spotted by a football expert from Spain. He approached they boy's parents and offered to send their boy to Spain to be enrolled in the football team. He also ensured that the boy's medical expenses would be paid by the management. The only condition was, if the boy was ready to move to Spain. The parents asked their kid and he agreed.

Now before I reveal the name of the boy, here is a wonderful quote by him:

"I start early and I stay late, day after day, year after year, it took me 17 years and 114 days to become an overnight success."

Last year this boy made $111 million. His current contract with FC Barcelona reportedly pays him $645,000 a week, or $33 million a year, through 2021. He has won the FIFA Player of the Year Award thrice. You might have guessed his name by now. His name is Lionel Messi.

Working hard the right way is what made this boy invincible. You might have heard that practice makes a man perfect. Let me modify it a bit, "Right practice makes a man perfect."

Therefore, discipline blended with hard work is the only key to harbor huge success and be known as a leader for the rest of your life.

CHAPTER 5

Make Your Land Prolific

Once there was a tiny seed named Sid that rested in the desert. While looking towards the sky, Sid would often wonder about the reason behind his existence. He pondered over the reason why he was dropped on earth. At times, mild wind would hide Sid under a mask of sand, while next morning he found himself exposed to direct sunlight. Sid could notice the same nature's play with other fellow seeds as well that were lying around.

One day a huge current of wind started to approach them. Sid and other seeds started to worry about their fate. Sid swirled and flew with the wind while being enveloped by sand, in one direction and then another. He tried with all his might to hide himself under the layers of sand but the wind was committed to dig all the escapers out. After being sucked by the wind for a couple of miles, Sid noticed himself spinning over the land covered with few towering trees and plantations. That sight invaded his eyes. Suddenly, he noticed the wind withdrawing its inescapable force and retreating back to mild breeze. Sid and the other seeds fell flat on their faces. They noticed the texture of the land was different than the sandy desert. This land had some waves of fragrance coming from the flowers. The birds were chirping and the squirrels were running around with nuts in their mouth that were of the same size as Sid's.

Sid decided to settle down and become like one of the huge tree that was home to many birds. Now this was unheard of in the desert. All the other seeds shouted:

"It can't be done!

It's never been done before!

It's impossible!"

Sid replied:

"Yes I can and I will prove it!"

Sid took no notice of what other seeds yelled at him and planted himself firmly in one spot. There lay Sid buried under tons of soil, waiting for some miracle to happen. After a few days, Sid noticed opening himself and sending up a little shoot and then sending down a little root. After another few days, Sid noticed tiny droplets of water falling from the sky. Sid shouted, "Oh, its rain, I have heard about the stories of rain from old seed that said it travelled from a far-off land. The water seemed to act as the growing tonic since Sid started to grow in size. The soil contributed to Sid's nourishment.

Years went by and Sid just grew bigger and bigger, stronger and stronger. Sid was amused to see new leaves and flowers budding on his branches. The flowers turned into fruits while dropping more seeds to the ground. Soon the new seeds also opened up and sent shoots up to the sky. In another few months, several little trees grew around Sid. Their roots had grown so deeply into the sand to find moisture that they started to suck water up to the surface. Soon, the land was moist enough to transform the area into grassland.

Now, there were several trees growing strong and tall. The water began to bubble to the surface and casted into a wonderful blue pond. Word about the pond was carried across by the wind. Little birds flew to see this spectacular place and make it their home. With them they carried all kinds of seeds which grew into beautiful plants and flowers that added a sparkle to that piece of land. Gradually people from across the world came to know about this newly-formed beautiful place. They would often come to enjoy the serenity and found themselves arrested in the sight of that terrain.

This is the end of the story. Now, just like in school, I am going to ask you the moral of the story. Yes, indeed, Sid was a brave and determined seed that added glistering beauty to that place. It was one seed that revolutionized that piece of land. But there is one more significant aspect that was responsible behind the head-turner change; the LAND! It was the land that turned the pea-sized seed into a tree. Sid was lying in the desert but its determination might not have helped him much had he not been transported to the fertile land.

Similarly, you might have the right plans, self-discipline and hard work in place. However, unless you do not work on polishing or acquiring the required **skillset/s**, you would not be able to grow into a tree of towering stature and inspire others.

"A winner is someone who recognizes his God-given talents, works his tail off to develop them into skills, and uses these skills to accomplish his goals."

—Larry Bird

Let's learn about how to make your land prolific. You might have heard the saying that skills can always be learnt. In terms of professional skills, in today's competitive and evolving world, where there are every-minute changes, one has to be on his toes to meet the criteria of 'survival of the fittest'. You are expected to be an expert in specific soft skills and hard skills or rather most of them.As a result, there is a herd of institutions running the training courses on these skills.You would often hear of every second institution offering course on some newly introduced skill. The other day when I was passing by, a hoarding caught my attention that read 'Learn how to impress your boss by working less?' I mean, there are courses available that teach you on skills that are neither fall in the hard nor the soft category.

Apart from professional life, there are certain skills that one needs to be exceptional in, like, relationship skill, communication skill, resilience skill, creative thinking skill and so on. However, a prerequisite to acquire all these skill is the *ability to learn those skills.* In the following section, we will walk through four skill sets that can prove to be useful in your professional as well as personal life. We can call them as **Life-Skills**.

1. Communication Skill

This is one skill that we engage in for most of our day. Every waking hour of our life involves the use of this skill. Upon waking up, most of us are in the habit of crawling our fingers to find our phone. We click on the messages, social media sites or emails and reply to some; we communicate. Then while getting ready, we talk to our wife, kids or parents; we communicate. After we leave for office, we look for a taxi or auto and bargain with the driver; we communicate. When we reach the office, we usually notice some fiery email from our boss asking for some explanation; we communicate. During break-time, we socialize with our colleagues; we communicate. We attend meetings or meet our clients; we communicate. Then while returning home, we receive a call from our home, asking to buy some grocery; we step in the store and again communicate. Upon returning home, we talk to our family members in a jovial or disturbed mood (depending on whether we had a smooth sail or we were raked over the coals in the office); we communicate. Finally, while trying to sleep, we try to summarize our whole day and sometimes even our life to ourselves; once again we communicate.

If you find it challenging to handle any of the above mentioned situations, then you need to rethink over enhancing your communication skill. Communication forms a significant part of our life and it is high time that we consider mastering this skill. It is the communication skill that gives us an edge over others. Here are some ways to master it:

- **Learn to Listen**: Everyone wants to be heard. Before you form an opinion or utter your words, listen to what the other person is saying. In case you have any doubts, do not hesitate to ask the other person to rephrase so as to avoid any misunderstandings. Interruptions or not letting the other person speak is something that is considered as unethical and this showcases a bad image of you.
- **Intensify your statements with appropriate Body Language**: This is generally influential in face-to-face meetings. When you are talking to someone, please don't be a news reader. You can infuse life in your words with relevant body gestures. Make sure you sit or stand with a straight spine and you use your hand gestures to make your statement more impactful. Another important aspect in body language is eye-contact. You should neither talk while looking at the end where the wall and ceiling meets; neither should you be looking unblinkingly with your eyeballs popped out. When you are communicating, ensure you have a mild smile on your face. This would make the other person feel valued and connected.

- **Make Notes wherever required**: Ensure that you carry with you a tidy notepad when you are going to meet your clients or attend a meeting. The other day I had to address a group of IT managers in an organization and I received a call from human resources asking if I needed anything specific. I told them about the make and model of my computer and asked them to let me know in case it was not compatible with their projector. On the presentation day, when I entered the conference hall only to I findout that my computer was not compatible with their projector. When I asked the HR personnel, she said, 'I forgot'. It was nothing but miscommunication on her part and to some extent on my part as well since I should have called her back for confirmation. There were certain slides that were an important part of the presentation and which were known only to my computer. My presentation could have broken beyond repair but thank God I always carry a drive as the backup. We transferred the file to one of the manager's computer and I got on with my talk.
- **Avoid Unnecessary Statements**: Always communicate in simple and precise words. If someone talks too much, the chances are likely that the person would go unnoticed or would be considered as an energy vampire. Few years back, when I was in the corporate world, there was a colleague who always had some or the other issue to talk over. Every day, upon entering the office,

his words used to be "this traffic is going to give me a heart attack" followed by "it's getting hotter and hotter every day." You say goodbye, he will drag you for a cup of coffee and spit his frustrations out. He is known as the venting-machine.

- **The Neutral Standpoint**: There are times when you are a in a group and all of a sudden the discussion takes a different turn. For instance, it might convert in some political wrath or criticizing someone and it might not be possible for you to find an escape route from the burning topic. During such times, even if you are in favor or not in agreement with others, it is advisable to maintain a neutral standpoint. Do not polarize yourself or it might result in conflicts at a later stage.

2. Decision-Making Skill

There are times when we find ourselves positioned at the crossroads, whether to take route one or route two or to retreat. Decision making is the key skill whether it is related to your workplace or personal life, and is particularly important if you want to be an effective leader. Each decision presents its own challenges, and we all have different ways of approaching problems. Where the world's top leaders are often spotted in formals, contrarily, successful businessmen such as Steve Jobs (black mock turtleneck and dad jeans), Mark Zuckerberg (gray T-shirt and hipster jeans), and Dilbert(white Sipowicz shirt and turnt-up tie) wore/wear similar clothes every day so that they have one less decision to make and thereby use that mental capacity for making better decisions.

No one can afford to make poor decisions. So, how do you avoid making bad decisions – or leave that to fate? You need a systematic approach to decision-making so that, no matter what type of decision you take,you attract positive outcome. Here are top 3 biases that usually cloud your judgment:

(i) Self-serving bias

In a survey, a group of people were asked which person would go to heaven and the choices were:

Bill Clinton	Princess Diana
Michael Jordan	Mother Teresa

79% percent people answered Mother Teresa, which was the highest score. However, a fifth option was added to the survey that read 'You'. This option was clicked by 87% of the people.

Generally, we take the credit of success on ourselves and blame the failure on the situations or others. This is the self-serving bias. For example, if we charm someone, it is because we have a charming personality and if we get rejected is because they don't deserve us. This in fact is a mechanism to shield our self-esteem. Such bias stops us from learning by our mistakes. If we don't take responsibility of our failures then we will not be able to take the initiative to change.

How to repair this self-serving bias?

Research shows that when you are with your close friends or family members, this self-serving bias disappears. Therefore, make sure you have friends and family members who keep you grounded.

(ii) Cognitive Fluency

Cognitive Fluency is, how easy an idea is to understand and implement. The more fluent is the idea, the more unconsciously we trust it. Here the problem is, whether something is easy, it has nothing to do with the truth. This leads to illusion of truth. Let's consider the below example:

This message is true

This message is true

Here, most people would choose the first sentence as true since it is more legible.

Therefore, next time, when you hear something that sounds blur, this is exactly when you should start questioning if you are keeping your finger on the right perspective.

(iii) Sunk Cost Fallacy

Imagine you have bought a movie ticket for the morning show but after one hour of watching, you think that the movie is of not of your taste. You want to leave but the thought that you spent money on the ticket and the snacks holds you back. This is the sunk cost fallacy.

Ideally, you have already lost the money that you invested. In fact, if you hold yourself back, you are wasting another precious hour of your life. Therefore, it is better to leave. It is recommended to evaluate the future cost and benefits before taking a decision and not cry over losses.

"Never lose good money over bad money."

—Unknown

Here are somemore steps that would help you to take constructive decision. So before you lock your decision:

- Evaluate how much time do you have (realistically)?
- Access the risk-reward ratio.
- Be honest with yourself, irrespective of domain that the decision revolves around.
- Opt for an outside perspective, which could be your friends, parents, wife, boss, colleague BUT at the same time trust yourself.
- You must have to access whether it is the right thing to do.
- You must need to conduct a cost/benefit analysis.
- To improve decision-making skills, you must need to trust your intuition.
- If the decision you took is proving to be bad, always have Plan B in place.

"Different perspectives, experiences and insights improve decision-making and lead to superior performance."

—Lynne Doughtie

3. Creative-Thinking Skill

Like all skills, even being able to think outside the box is a learnable skill. Creative imagination can help get you think outside of the proverbial box.You just have to be willing to try new things. A great way to improve your creative thinking skills is to improve the diversity and quality of our experiences. Here are 5 ways that can help awake and polish the creative thinker inside you:

- **Try new things**

  By trying new things, we gain new experiences. Listen to a genre of music you would ordinarily never listen to. Watch some movies you would normally scoff at. Take up a hobby you have never considered. Forcing yourself into experiencing the world in new ways helps you be more creative and imaginative.By having a diversity of experiences, you have more building blocks to build your imagination with.

- **Continuous Learning**

  Both creativity and innovation are based on knowledge.Therefore, you need to continually expand your knowledge base. Read things you don't normally read as often as you can.

- **Observe with all senses**

  Truly, creative people have developed their ability to observe and to use all of their senses, which can get dull over time.Take time to "sharpen the blade" and take everything in. Add thoughts as you go.

- **Eat differently**

  There are studies upon studies that discuss how our diet affects the way we think. Want to start thinking differently? Start giving your body different (and healthier) fuel. You would be shocked how much more creatively you can think and act when you eat a healthier diet.Remember, you are what you eat

- **Do the "No Bad Ideas Brainstorming" exercise**

  Get at least one other person to join you for a 45-60 minute brainstorming session. No technology and no criticism whatsoever. Bring a topic or idea you want to brainstorm to the table, and just start pitching it back and forth. Write down all your ideas (on actual paper) and don't critique a single idea. It's important to do this in person and to make absolutely sure you don't have any negative energy or feedback throughout the process. You may end up with 100 horrible ideas, but I bet you will have one or two good ones. Plus, you will get better at this the more you do it.

You don't have to be a creative thinker to be able to think outside the box, you just need to take more initiatives that stimulate creative thinking. Even the most creative people need help getting inspired.

"Dance above the surface of the world.
Let your thoughts lift you into creativity
that is not hampered by opinion."

—Red Haircrow

4. Take the Lead Skill

Well, this book is about kindling the leader inside you. Therefore, never hesitate to take the lead whenever you get the opportunity. Besides, where there is no opportunity available, ***create one***! Set yourself apart from the ordinary person or employee and be noticed as a future leader ahead of your peers. How do you set yourself apart so that you will be identified for career success ahead of others? With a few consistent actions you can develop your leadership potential. Here are 4 ways to get noticed as an upcoming-leader, one who is a key member of the team:

1. Be a team player

According to the Center for Creative Leadership's World Leadership Survey, organizations prefer leaders who are collaborative, inclusive and team-oriented. Helping your team deal with conflict, develop cohesion and work together will quickly set you apart to team leaders and managers.

2. Lead from where you are

A leader isn't always identified by a title. One of the most difficult things to do but something that will get you noticed is 'leading while not formally in charge'. Taking extra initiatives and difficult tasks will get you noticed by your managers. Eventually, when it's time for managers to move on to other opportunities, they will likely think of you first as the right one to take charge of their position.

3. Be an expert but learn and master new skills

Performing well in your current role is an excellent way to get noticed. After that, look around and identify what additional skills and jobs you can master. Stay on the top of changes in your career field. Senior managers will notice people who have already demonstrated the willingness and aptitude to perform at a higher level, and who are eager to learn.

4. Be open to feedback and criticism, rather use it to grow

Ask your senior for corrective feedback. It might be difficult but it demonstrates that you are not only comfortable with your abilities, but that you take your career growth seriously and are willing to learn from mistakes. When you are criticized or you make a mistake, own it. Ask your senior to describe what the right approach would have been so you have a clear expectation of what they would have done had they been in your shoes.

Friends, as mentioned before, learning is an ever-ending process. We often come across the need to magnify a particular skill depending on the situation; however, we often place that initiative on the backburner. Life still moves on even if we procrastinate. Had Sid also decided to leave it to fate, it would have still been lying dormant on the surface with the fellow seeds. And the wonderful creation would not have sprouted. This is the right time to analyze the skills that you need to develop to propel yourself and start working on them. Take the accountability of your life and prove your capability to the rest of the world. Believe me; you have what all it takes to become a trendsetter! In case you find it challenging to make the grade, look for a mentor who is a maestro in that skill. This is how you equip yourself to play the winning shot!

Happy Skill Learning and Polishing!

CHAPTER 6

Do Not Let the Wick of Confidence Fade Away

Let's begin this chapter with another inspiring story but this time I would not keep the suspense. This is the story of Jack Ma, the co-founder and chairman of the Alibaba Group. Jack Ma has impacted the entire economy and the Internet industry of China almost single-handedly. He is today one of the most valued leaders of the world. However, the Jack Ma, we know today, was all together a different identity few years back. Rather let's begin with his childhood days.

Born to traditional musician story-teller parents on October 15, 1964 in Hangzhou, China, Jack Ma was the second child (out of three) in the family. However, his zeal to enhance his aptitude and acquire new skills was evident from childhood. From the year 1972 tourism boomed in his city and the spirited Jack made the most of the opportunity. He worked as a tourist guide in exchange for lessons in English. Apparently, he became good friend of a tourist who named him as Jack since his original name was difficult to be pronounced. The two continued correspondence further.

However, his education was not a smooth sail. Jack failed in his primary school examinations twice, but this did not let the wick of his confidence fade away. In the middle school, he again failed thrice but still the wick of his confidence stayed ignited.

Well, this was not the end of his failures during academics. When he was in high school, he applied to various universities and failed in the entrance exam thrice. His confidence was still unblemished. He wanted to join Harvard University but he got rejected 10 times; still unwavering confidence. Eventually, in his third attempt, he joined the Hangzhou Dianzi University, where he graduated with a Bachelor in English.

After graduating from college, he applied for 30 different jobs and was rejected by all of them. He even applied for the post of a police officer but they did not give him the time of the day. They rejected him saying 3 words "You're no good". Had anyone been in his shoes, one would have felt defeated in life but this man was packed to the brim with confidence. He relied on his English and got appointed as a teacher in a local university he had attended a few years ago. Later, he started a translation service business.

During his first visit in 1995 to U.S, as a translator, Jack got introduced to the Internet. He was completely aghast after he entered the keyword 'beer' and learnt there was not a single Chinese beer manufacturer listed. Jack immediately evaluated the potential opportunities of Internet in his country of a billion people. He thought of connecting China to the rest of the world. Eventually, he and his friends decided to launch a website about China and Chinese products known as 'chinapage' that listed Chinese businesses. Within the same day, they began to receive emails from people around the world, requesting them to partner with their company. That experience taught Jack about the incredible power of connectivity, especially how the Internet can impact the global trade essentially for small medium enterprises.

However, due to lack of funding, Jack had to shut down this business. Again, his wick of confidence still did not fade away. He later took up a government job for a short period. There he built important connections with important people, which later impacted his life and business venture. One of the associates was a founding member of Yahoo, Jerry Yang. In 1999, after leaving the government job, Jack took a second bite at the Internet-based business ventures by grouping 18 people including himself and his wife. He sold them the dream about Alibaba with the goal of facilitating international trade for small and medium ventures based in China.

In the early stages of Alibaba, Jack tried to raise funds from Silicon Valley, but he was again met with denial and his business model was criticized to be unprofitable and unsustainable by many during that time. Once again, the wick of his confidence was still aflame.

Not the one to get bowed down easily, Jack continued his efforts to raise funds and eventually Jack was successful in getting Goldman Sachs and Soft Bank to invest $25 million in Alibaba. Later, as the .com boom period came to a screeching halt in the year 2000, Alibaba faced serious challenges due to its aggressive expansion in the international market. Jack Ma; the man confident of his success, prudently reorganized companies and operations, including closing many international branches and focusing on strengthening Alibaba's position in the Chinese market.

Thereafter, Jack expanded the services of Alibaba and reengaged its international expansion strategy. Ultimately, Jack was able to drive eBay out of China after just few years of being in business. Jack succeeded in getting Yahoo to invest the size of 1 billion dollars for a 40% stake in Alibaba.

Later in 2014, what turned out to be largest IPO in the world till date, Jack and his team successfully raised in access of 25 billion dollars for Alibaba by listing it in the New York Stock Exchange. That made Alibaba, a 15 years old ecommerce company that has its origins outside of the U.S as one of the world's largest company as measured by market capitalization, that was approximately 200 billion dollars.

Well, even after achieving so much, Jack feels that there is still a long way to go ahead. Even today Jack's company has been acquiring many small size and mid-size companies and expanding in size.

If a boy from such a humble background, in spite of a series of failures, can grow to be one of the world's richest men by having faith in himself, anyone can.

I reiterate, 'Do not let the wick of your confidence fade away'!

"The most beautiful thing you can wear is confidence."

—Blake Lively

Let us learn more about self-confidence. Self-confidence is how we feel about ourselves. We generally tend to be most confident when we look good, feel accomplished and feel supported. However, one of the uphill tasks is to feel confident when you are not feeling that way. The good news is, there are many things you can do to elevate how you feel about yourself, which in turn will improve your confidence. Here are 9 simple tricks to help you elevate your confidence:

1. ***Take care of yourself***: Self-confidence depends on a combination of good physical, emotional and social health. It is hard to feel good about yourself if do not like your physique or constantly have low energy. Take out time to cultivate good exercise, eating and sleeping habits. Besides, dress the way you want to feel and not what others want you to

resemble. Feel the self-confidence by making the effort to look after your own needs.

2. ***Visualize yourself as you want to be***: Our self-image means so much to us, often more than we realize. We have a mental picture of ourselves and it determines how confident we feel. When we struggle with low self-confidence, we have a poor perception of ourselves that is often inaccurate and governed by situations. Visualization is the technique of seeing an image of yourself that you are proud of, in your own mind. So practice the best version of yourself.
3. ***Improve your posture***: Posture plays a huge role in feeling and looking confident. Standing tall with your chest out and shoulders back, showcases confidence, and can even trick you into feeling more confident. Try to imagine a string coming out the top of your head pulling you into an upright position. This will help you look taller and broader, while in the process making you feel more confident and capable.
4. ***Affirm yourself***: We tend to behave in accordance with our own self-image. The trick to make a lasting change, is to change how you view yourself. We believe whatever we tell ourselves constantly and affirmations are positive and uplifting statements that we say to ourselves. For example, if you don't like something about your physical appearance, practice saying something that you appreciate

or like about yourself when you look in the mirror. We will learn more about affirmations in Chapter 8.

5. ***Put in the work***: It's hard to be confident when you don't think you will do well at something. Beat that feeling by preparing yourself as much as possible. Irrespective of the challenge, you need to know what you are doing and how to face it boldly. To be confident in something, you need to practice it. No one ever felt confident doing something for the first time, the tenth time or even the hundredth time.
6. ***Redefine fear and failure***: Your relationship with fear and failure can hold you back and cause your self-confidence to plummet. To help prevent this from happening, you need to change the way you think about fear and failure. Try to see fear as the opportunity to progress and failure as the chance to gather valuable feedback on what you need to work on. By doing this, fear and failure become tools for progression, instead of reasons of not to do something.
7. ***Empower yourself with knowledge***: Empowering yourself, in general, is one of the best strategies to build self-confidence. You can do this in many ways, but one of the best ways to empower yourself is through knowledge. By becoming more knowledgeable, you will be more confident… and you become more knowledgeable by doing

research and studying. You can find information on Internet, read books or take courses. You can also learn from people around you who have done what you want to achieve.

8. ***Embody confidence***: Whenever you find yourself out of your comfort zone- whether by chance or choice, stop for moment! Close your eyes and think of the time when you felt confident and self-assured. Use all your senses to bring yourself back to that moment. By doing this, you will be more able to cultivate that feeling in the present moment. Or, just think about how a confident person would act in that situation, and do what they would do! You will be amazed at how soon you will find yourself feeling confident and capable.
9. ***Smile***: You might have heard this one a thousand times and even once earlier in this book (under the topic 'appropriate body language') but it really does work! We all are social beings and we thrive on social interactions. Specifically, positive social interaction. It can make us feel happy, confident and content. Think about how your mood changes when someone smiles back at you, or even how it changes when you crack and smile to yourself. So next time you feel low in self-confidence, try smiling. It will make you feel a lot better!
10. Confidence plays a vital role in your ability to achieve success and happiness in your professional as well as personal life. It affects almost everything

you do, from what you think, to what you say, and even how you look. By using these tips, you can learn how to be confident in almost any situation and start going after the things you want most in life.

Friends, confidence is a positive thing that can be boosted by self-care,eating healthy, self-talk, never give up attitude. Change your though patterns to positive by reading, learning and visualizing your thoughts. Last but not the least, always keep smiling since you are on the way to become a leader that others can look up to!

"With confidence, you have won before you have started."

—Marcus Garvey

CHAPTER 7

Stress-Free All 365 Days

If there is one word everyone knows these days it's stress management. Well, rather two words.The world is bombarded with books, courses and information available online about stress management. Generally, our ears are instructed to take care of stress. However, are we not supposed to take care of things that are precious to us, like, our family, our work or business, our financial needs and assets? Why would someone want to manage stress? Factually and unknowingly, we have formed an opinion that stress is a part of our body, just like other body parts. Stress seems to be turning into a chronic ailment that we unable to get rid of.

However, there is one fact that we all should embed in our mind that stress is not a part of us. We get stressful because we do not know how to handle our mind. No attention has been paid as to how to handle this mind, how to handle this emotion, how to handle this body and how to handle the energies that we have been accorded with. We somehow tend to manage such a sophisticated system accidentally. Therefore, stress is a natural outcome of such unconscious living.

It is not your job or your life situation or relationship which is stressful. Stress is spreading its mantle on you because of your inability or conscious awareness to manage. To put it in plain words, 'not knowing how to manage is stressfulness'. If things would have happened the way you wanted, you would not have been stressful. This stress has made us an easy prey for several ailments both mentally and physically. Let us first understand how stress injects its fangs and drains our health.

Stress is a feeling we all experience when we are challenged or overwhelmed. But more than just an emotion, stress is a hardwired physical response that travels through your entire body. In the short term, stress can be advantageous, but when activated too often or too long, your primitive 'fight of flight' stress response not only changes your brain but also damages many of the other organs and cells throughout your body.

Your adrenal gland releases the stress hormones known as adrenalin and norepinephrine. As these hormones travel through your blood stream, they easily reach your blood vessels and heart. Adrenalin causes your heart to beat faster and raises your blood pressure over time, causing hypertension. Together, these changes increase the chances of heart attack, stroke and many other fatal diseases. By this I do not mean to scare you. My simple intention is to share the mechanism of stress and suggest you ways to break-free from stress.

Let's say, you drive your car at 2000 RPM, the engine may last about a hundred thousand miles. If you drive the same engine at 5000 RPM, it may last only fifty thousand miles or less. Similarly, least the amount of friction in your life, the smoother your life would be. You would be able to get more in life, with least amount of stress.

There is one regime that most of us have been entangled in; the social media and electronic messaging. This entanglement is not only adding anxiety but is also degrading the quality of our life and relationships. Every day, we receive messages and friend requests from people whom we don't even know or who are not close to us.We copy a forwarded message just for the sake of replying. Even the birthdays and anniversaries are now slip-wished with text messages and fancy copied images. If we message or call someone and we do not hear back (even for formality sake), we feel angry. There are chances that the other person might be busy but we assume that we are being ignored and start plotting. It has become this easy for us to throw someone out from our life. This way, are we not compromising not only with the quality of our life but even the time that we could have otherwise spent with our family, friends and most importantly with ourselves?

I was travelling on a train last week and a husband and wife with two kids were sitting next to me. I was surprised to see that they were carrying four phones (maybe some more in the luggage), one for each.The smallest kid, had his teeth sunk in the mobile screen, with the father looking very proud. After a while, the battery of one of the kid's phone died on him. That opened the Pandora's Box as the rest, started fighting over who would share the phone now.

That was something which made me ponder over our dependency on bootless mediums. I remember, when I was a kid, travelling with parents was something that always excited me. I used to keep asking my parents about everything that went by. However, all such delightful sights are not known to most of the kids of today. We might have hundreds of friends added to our Facebook account but no one to talk to when we need. Such futile engagements in our daily life have heightened the stage of anxiety.

Hence, it is the right time to do some 'Inner Engineering' and show an exit route to the factors that cause stress. Let's learn the ropes about this stress because until we are not aware, we would not be able to uproot this evil from our lives.

Good Stress VS Bad Stress

We all know stress by the name of a celebrated villain but do you know that stress could be good at times? Good stress is what motivates us to achieve our goal, whereas, bad stress is something that affects our mental and physical health. Let's say a lion is chasing a deer in the midst of aforest range in Africa. The mighty cat has injected all its energy to get closer to the deer. On the other hand, the deer is also running on its full tilt to escape the deadly jaws. Here, the lion is under good stress because the chances are likely that it will be able to chase down the dear and earn the breakfast treat. Contrarily, the deer is under bad stress because the chances are likely that it would be served to the lion. Here I am reminded of a quote that I would like to share with you:

> *"Every morning in Africa, a gazelle wakes up. It knows it must run faster than the fastest lion or it will be killed. Every morning a lion wakes up. It knows it must outrun the slowest gazelle or it will starve to death. It doesn't matter whether you are a lion or a gazelle: when the sun comes up, you'd better be running."*
>
> **—*Christopher McDougall***

Therefore, not all stress is bad for you. If nothing in life causes any stress or excitement, you may start to live a monotonous life and not live up to your potential. As they say, "If the road is smooth and everything is coming your way, it means you are in the wrong lane."

Here, let me turn the tables by sharing something. The good news is that since we humans are superior to all other species on the earth, therefore, we have the capability to transform bad stress into good stress. How? Let me cite an example from the incident that happened with my friend. I am going to narrate this event in the same words he did.

"Some time back I went to Kalimpong in West Bengal, India. Although heights scare me but I decided to get a bird's eye view of the Kanchenjunga river, that is, by paragliding. It is said that it is one of the most memorable landmarks that invades your heart.

The moment I trekked to the lush green hill top, I felt scared of jumping from such a high point. I was reminded of the movie 'Vertical Limit'. The turbo speed of the wind almost ballooned the clothes I was wearing. After noticing some paragliders diving in the valley, I decided to give up the idea of adding the crowning glory to the book of my life. I had travelled that far to enjoy the cherished dream of my life but the bad stress forced me to retreat. Suddenly I noticed a small girl wearing her jumping gear and getting ready to take a plunge in the lap of nature. It was not that she was not scared but her ear-to-ear smile and a sparkle in her eyes were more prominent. She was waving her parents who also looked a little feared but more of excited to see their daughter paraglide. Finally, she waved her hand and started running to gain momentum. Within seconds, she was seen splitting through the waves of air, like an eagle soaring high and enjoying the glide.

That was a moment of self-realization for me. I immediately stopped fostering my bad stress and decided to take the sky-touching stride of my life. As I elevated several hundred feet above the ground and started enjoying the awe-inspiring glide, my bad stress evaporated completely. I felt the adrenalin rush gushing and invading every single cell of my body. I felt prideful of having taken the decision to overcome my fear where that girl acted as a strong trigger."

Hence, there are times when the situation is under your control and you can make efforts to cease the bad stress. However, sometimes the situation is not under your control or you cannot do much about the problem. During such times, stay calm and enjoy the glide!

"The ultimate measure of a man is not where he stands in moments of comfort and convenience, but where he stands at times of challenge and controversy."

—Martin Luther King, Jr.

What is the First Step to Remodel Bad Stress into Good Stress?

Friends, the first and most important step to transmute bad stress into good stress is to '*self-realize that you are under bad stress*'. You should be on the lookout for the signs that your life is being adversely affected by bad stress.

Let us find out some ways to find out if you are trapped in the clutches of bad stress:

- If you have memory problems, you thoughts are always racing, you are constantly worrying and you frequently make bad decisions; these are the signs of bad stress.
- If you are facing problems controlling your moods, you increasingly have a short temper, you find it hard to relax and you feel lonely; bad stress could be feasting on you.

- If you experience several aches and pains and you are suffering from dizziness, nausea or bowel issues, you have lost your sex drive or have frequent colds; it could be the bad stress on play.
- If your eating habits have changed, you are sleeping for extended hours or too little, you want to spend more time alone, you don't seem to be able to complete projects on time, you start drinking or smoking to relax or even using drugs; it's time to show the outside door to bad stress.

If you are experiencing most or all of these symptoms, then I would recommend you to stop here and visit a doctor to get yourself checked for depression. However, if only few symptoms have surfaced at some time or the other, then take it as a wakeup call. It is time to free yourself from the embrace of bad stress. Let's learn about some proven ways to beat bad stress out of your life:

- *Let Nature declutter your mind*: It has been proved that the time spent in Nature or even a simple house plant can lower the bad stress levels. In 1982, the Japan government started a ShinrinYoku campaign. It involved promoting the benefits of spending time in the forest to dilute bad stress. In just one short visit to the forest, the cortisol levels, heart rate and blood pressure were shown to decrease. Even hospital patients, who have a view of nature, tend to have better pain tolerance and faster recovery rates compared to those who faced only a blank wall. Even preparing tea with fresh tea leaves is said to have worked miraculously to overcome bad stress.

- *Let music abolish the bad stress*: Like nature, music can have a similar effect. Songs with 60 to 80 beats per minute but no lyrics have been shown to reduce stress even in patients who have undergone various types of surgeries.There is no better time to play your kind of music than the moment you wake up. And the music should be played subtly. This is never the kind of music that booms and wakes everyone up.Try playing something more mellow. This should ease you through the day by setting you in a good mood first thing in the morning, a good way to kill stress with music.
- *Deep Breaths; the stress busters*: Whenever you feel bad stress taking a toll on you, just stop for a second and breathe deeply. When you inhale, feel the breath travelling from your nose to throat, to the lungs and to the navel. Again while exhaling, feel the breath moving up from your navel, to your lungs, throat and finally expelling while gently touching the walls of your nostrils. Feel that the bad stress is being emitted out of your body as you exhale. Try to relax, let your shoulders fall down, and try to eliminate any tension in your jaw and face. You will quickly feel the bad stress vanishing and you would feel energized. This is something that's incredibly easy and simple to do in whatever situation you are in, either at home, during a

stressful day at work, at a school exam or when having to deal with an urgent situation.

- *Add smiles in real life*: Again, smile is something that finds in place in every moment of your life, irrespective of the situations. They say, laughter is the best medicine, which also turns out to be the best stress medicine. When we laugh, our oxygen intake increases, stimulating the release of endorphins. Studies even show that simply waiting to see a funny movie can increase the beta endorphin levels by 27% and decrease the bad stress hormone levels in the bloodstream. After watching a side-splitting movie, the participant (during research) had lower levels of bad stress hormone. They experienced the feeling of attachment, bonding, contentment and felt secure.

  A smile ranging from a mild lift of lips to a cheek-to-cheek grin would be the perfect way, starting from the beginning of the day till the time you retire in bed. It is said 'fake it till you make it'. So even if you have to wear a fake smile in the beginning, that's fine. Besides, if during any moment of the day, you find your smile turning into an ear-splitting laugh, do not hesitate to laugh your lungs out. Just stay happy!

Friends, it is not that bad stress should not surface in our lives. At times, even the toughest of the men find themselves encircled under the black clouds of back-breaking stress. What matters is self-awareness followed by the initiative to refashion bad stress into favorable (good) stress. This is what sets apart a leader from a mediocre person.

Every day is Friday! Time to recast your bad stress into GOOD stress!

CHAPTER 8
Miracle of Affirmations

Affirmations are the positive words that you repeat to yourself over and over to nurture your mind to achieve things that you actually want. Affirming is a powerful tool that encourages self-empowerment and the practice of positive thinking. Affirming is the way you direct your mind to work in a particular way or towards a particular goal. These are based upon the beliefs of the power of the spoken word or sentence. It is a tool to communicate with yourself. What you speak, your mind, your emotions and your body will believe it.

There are times when you are striving to achieve a goal. However, in the back of your mind you foster fear 'what if I fail' and it actually comes true. There could be times when you might have missed by a hair's breath. Why? It is because you have been feeding your mind with the fear of failure, although unknowingly. As a result, your mind starts to believe in that fear and starts working to convert it into a reality.

According to the Journal of Projective Techniques in 1957, Dr. Philip West was treating Mr. Wright, who was suffering from advanced cancer, lymphosarcoma. In spite of every advanced treatment, no improvement was seen and the case was being seen as hopeless. The condition of Mr. Wright was critical. Dr. West did not expect him to last a week.

However, Mr. Wright desperately wanted to live. Upon hearing about the new drug Krebiozen, which was being studied, he insisted his doctor to treat him with the new drug. Unfortunately, the drug was only being offered to people in clinical trials who were believed to have at least three months left to live. Mr. Wright was too sick to qualify.

Mr. Wright begged so hard, however, the doctor decided to give him one injection on Friday. Even though the doctor secretly suspected that Mr. Wright would not last the weekend, Mr. Wright had a belief in the miracle cure.

The following Monday, Dr. West found his patient walking around, out of bed. After receiving the injection, the patient's tumors began receding "like snowballs on a hot stove" and were half their original size.

Mr. Wright was enjoying his life, praising Krebiozen as a miracle drug until a few months later, however, a newspaper article published the results of the study showing that the drug was worthless. Mr. Wright, who trusted what he read in the literature, lost all his faith in his treatment, fell into a deep depression and his cancer came back.

This time Dr. West, who genuinely wanted to help and save his patient, decided to get sneaky. He told Mr. Wright that some of the initial supplies of the drug had deteriorated during shipping, making them less effective, but that he scored a new batch of highly concentrated, ultra-pure Krebiozen, which he could give him.

In what might now be viewed as unethical practice, the doctor gave Mr. Wright another treatment and assured him that it was a new, more potent form of the drug; in reality, the injection contained only distilled water. Surprisingly, the tumors again melted away, the fluid in his chest disappeared, and Mr. Wright was feeling great again for another two months.

Then the American Medical Association blew it by announcing that a nation wide study of Krebiozen proved that the drug was utterly worthless. This time, Mr. Wright lost all faith in his treatment. His cancer came right back, and he died two days later.(Reference- *"The Psychobiology of Mind-Body Healing - New Concepts of Therapeutic Hypnosis"* by Ernest Lawrence Rossi)

Here, the negative affirmations treaded Mr. Wrightto the door of death. Earlier, even the injections filled with distilled water seemed to work wonders but the moment he started communicating to his mind about the ill-effects, he invited Mr. Death. Similarly, you can use positive affirmation to transpire a positive change in your life. You can become a magnet to your goals. Affirmations support your mental attitude and by reciting affirmations, it will give you the power to achieve success in whatever you want. By beginning the practice of recitingaffirmations, you will start to notice a drastic change in your life. However, while practicing affirmations, deliberately or unknowingly, there are some mistakes that we make and this is what makes all the difference. Here are some suggestions to make affirmations actually work for you.

"You will be a failure, until you impress your subconscious with the conviction you are a success. This is done my making an affirmation which 'clicks'.

—Florence Scovel Shinn

Suggestions to Make Affirmations Work for You

No Affirmations with a knot, sorry 'NOT'!

One day, it so happened that a man went to the village astrologer to find a solution to some problem he was facing in life. The astrologer suggested him some remedies that were to be implied simultaneously. While narrating the last remedy, the astrologer said, "Do not think of a monkey" or the remedies would not work (probably the astrologer was not sure of the treatment he offered, so he played smart). The man left the astrologer's home. On his way back, he noticed a monkey sitting at the roof of one of the houses and grinning at him. He ignored that monkey.

Upon reaching the split road, he noticed a group of monkeys crossing the road. He again reminded himself not to think of monkeys. Not much time passed by when the man started seeing monkeys driving the car, riding in the bus and selling bananas. Suddenly, the man noticed a group of monkeys running towards him. The man gathered all the guts he had and ran at the lightning speed towards his house. Upon reaching his house, he pushed the bell switch while huffing and puffing heavily. When the door was opened, to his surprise, he found a monkey had answered the door, who was actually his wife.

Similarly, in practical life, we generally practice affirmation by affixing it with a NOT. For example, 'we should **not** give up', 'I will **not** waste any more time', 'I will **not** drive fast', I will **not** skip my morning walk' and so on. Our subconscious mind does not understand the language of 'no'. This increases the chances for the mind to focus more on what you instructed not to focus on.

Quote Affirmations in 'Present Tense'

Do not use 'I will' or 'I might', instead say 'I am', 'I have' because our mind does not know the difference between what we imagine and what we experience. Therefore, the more NOW you can incorporate, the more likely it is to come into your life. When we boldly state that what we want is already ours, the Universe conspires to make it happen.

Evaluate before you affirm

I came across a client who came to me and said that he had been affirming since last six months and not even a leaf had moved. He was preparing for the engineering entrance exam. Ultimately, he was not able to clear the entrance exam that he had been preparing for since months. He said that he had affirmed for all those months.

Upon further counseling, it was revealed that it was his parents who wanted him to be an engineer, although he wanted to opt for MBA in finance. Therefore, he affirmed and burnt the midnight oil while preparing for the exam but nothing worked since his mind was not convinced. Hence, before you affirm, ensure that you are asking for what you want and not what others want.

Speak out loud

Remember, in school, during our exam days, we were often found reading the chapters loud so that our mind could register them. Similarly, you need to speak the affirmations loud to get the affirmation soaked by your mind. Ideally, reciting for five minutes, three times a day would be fine, that is, upon waking up, afternoon and while sleeping. Another option that helps to reinforce the new belief and would be easy to do is, to scribble down the affirmation several times in a notebook. Notice over time as you write it if your style of writing changes. This could be a clue as to how your mind perceives the new concept.

Get a friend or coach to repeat your affirmation to you

As they (friend or coach) are saying, for example, "You are remarkable and cherished," identify this statement as 'you are a wonderful person', 'you are amazing' and so on messages. If you don't have someone whom you feel comfortable asking, then use your reflection in the mirror as the person who is reinforcing the healthy message.

Here are some affirmations that could help you in the respective areas:

- **Affirmations for Good Health**

  "I am ready to enjoy perfect health!"

  "An endless supply of healing energy streams through me at all times!"

  "I attract pure health and wellness every day!"

  "I love exercising and eating healthy foods!"

  "I take care of my body with respect and love!"

  "I am known for my positive energy and healthy lifestyle!"

- **Affirmations to Attract Happiness**

  "Happiness is my natural state!"

  "Every day in every way I am getting happier and happier!"

  "Every new day starts with happiness, is full of joy and ends with contentment!"

  "I touch many lives. My happiness makes everyone happy, thus making it a happy world!"

  "I enjoy every moment of the day!"

  "For me happiness is a journey, not a destination!"

  "I am creating the life I deserve to live!"

  "I give myself permission to be happy!"

- **Affirmations to Become a Wealth Magnet**

  "Money is good, I adore money!"

  "Money is a free-flowing energy that keeps coming to my life!"

  "I am a money magnet!"

  "There is no limit to the amount of money I am capable of earning!"

  "If other people have become rich, I too can!"

  "There is plenty of money in the Universe and there is plenty for me."

  "It feels so good to have so much money!"

- **Affirmations to Prosper in Relationships**

  "I give and receive love freely and joyfully!"

  "I find love everywhere I go. Life is amazing!"

  "I love being with people who bring out the best in me!"

  "I accept that I am infinitely loved!"

  "I love everyone and in turn everyone loves me!"

- **Affirmations to Attract Success!**

  "Being successful is my natural state of being!"

  "All my actions are aimed at reaching my goals. I achieve my goals one after another!"

  "I am a solution oriented person. All problems are solvable!"

  "I always spot opportunities and utilize them. New doors are always opening for me!"

"I am in charge of my emotions, desires and abilities. I focus only on success!"

"I realize that success is a result of right thinking and hard work. I excel in both!"

Affirmations have the ability to rewire your brain. Then why not use them in your favor instead of against you? The all-time greatest boxer Muhammad Ali was a strong believer in affirmation. Before every match, while in the dressing room, he would affirm to himself that he has already won the match. He used to visualize himself celebrating his victory after the match. As a result, the great Ali shattered several records and became the world heavyweight champion winning 56 of 61 fights.

"It's the repetition of affirmations that leads to belief. And once that belief becomes a deep conviction, things begin to happen."

—Muhammad Ali

Experts estimate that an average mind hatches around 50,000 thoughts a day. That's an average of 2100 thoughts per hour. Isn't that incredible? These thoughts get registered in our mind by way of affirmations. However, it is a fact that most of the thoughts are negative. To put it in other words, there are 50,000 thoughts between us and our success or failure. We may not have control over our thoughts but we certainly have the control to turn most (if not all) of the thoughts into positive statements. And the most effective tool that every single leader follows is, by feeding the mind with positive affirmations. This way they program their mind for success! Hence, make positive affirmations the food for your thought.

Words have the power to change our life; words have the power to motivate and empower us to achieve what we want. Break-free from the bubble of negative communication with your mind and write your own destiny! Here is a simple and the master-key affirmation that you can practice every day and notice the magical change by your self.

"I am a born leader! I am a source
of inspiration to others!"

CHAPTER 9

Stop Sulking; Be Grateful to Magnetize More Success

When you wake up, what is the first thing you do? Probably, check your phone? Have tea? After we leave for office, we commit ourselves to our work, seniors and clients. Then at night, we try to think of the day gone by, whether it was like a cake walkor it was like a fly in the face of challenges. If some day trespasses our limit of handling the challenges, we blame our destiny or people or even the Almighty for obvious reasons.

Unfortunately, during this whole drill, we forget one person; our own Self. Friends, you are the most important piece of life in your life. Then why don't we pay some attention to ourselves? Why do we take ourselves as granted? There are a million people who went to bed last night and who will not wake up tomorrow morning. Tomorrow if you are able to hear the milkman knocking at your door, is it not a fantastic thing? So, the first thing you should do when you wake up is smile, thank the Almighty for adding to your lifeline. Thank the sunlight leaking from the curtains to have kissed your skin for yet another day. Then while eating your food, thank the nature for making food available for you. Unfortunately, one in every six people on earth does not get enough food to live a healthy life.While you are making your bed to sleep, thank the Universe for empowering you with the achievements and for the learning (failures). This is what we call as the '*attitude of gratitude*'. Nothing is more honorable than a grateful heart.

Gratitude is the healthiest of all human emotions. The more you express gratitude for what you have, the more likely you will have even more to express gratitude for. If you aim at nothing, you will hit it every time. Don't join an easy crowd, you won't grow. Again, 'if you do the same things, you will get the same results. If you want different results, you need to do the same things differently.' Go where the expectations and the demands to perform are high.

"Gratitude is a powerful process for shifting your energy and bringing more of what you want in your life. Be grateful for what you already have and you will attract more good things."

—'The Secret' by Rhonda Byrne

Learn how to be happy with what you have while you pursue all that you are aiming for. We may not laugh on the same joke on the second time but we keep crying over the same problem again and again. Yet your mind keeps going to those areas where there are problems. "It is necessary, therefore, for all of us that we focus on the good that is happening in our life and 'deal' with the bad or problems that are happening in our life." Let us not consume our minds with negativity. Let us focus on the positive and deal with the negative. Count your many blessings and name them one by one. You will be surprised with what you have. There are so many good things you might not have imagined.

> *"Gratitude is the attitude that gives us the fortitude to deal with the toughest challenges in our lives."*
>
> **—Gaur Gopal Das**

Here are 5 ways that can help you unleash the hidden power of gratitude and manifest your desires:

1. **Capacity to live in the present moment**

   When you are grateful, you find yourself fully present in the current moment. It's like waking up from a daze to discover a treasure right before you. It is like shining the torch on something that has been there for quite some time but you never noticed before. Most people spend their lives while being caught between memories of the past or worries about the future. As a result, they end up sleep walking through their days, weeks and years of life.

2. **Be connected**

   Experiencing gratitude allows you to connect with yourself, your surrounding and people in your life. When you practice gratitude regularly, you start to discover what really matter to you. You begin to realize what touches your heart, what inspires you to accomplish what you really care about the most. Your life begins to feel richer as you become aware of the smaller things that you already have that make life truly worth living. You begin to appreciate the people in your life. You become more understanding and develop greater empathy for others. You realize that you are not alone. You begin to see just how much help and support you actually do receive from others without even realizing it. It allows you to connect with something greater than yourself. You notice synchronicities in your daily life. You start to notice how unrelated things begin to connect in unexpected ways. You may find that you can reach flow states and accomplish your dreams easier than you did in the past.

3. **A new dimension to your perspectives**

   Gratitude changes your perspective. So much of our lives are spent struggling, trying to accomplish goals and dealing with relationships. We consistently live in a state or are trying to be somewhere or someone else. When you focus on what you don't have or what you believe is missing in your life, it's easy to feel tired or discouraged. The color drains out of life and all you see are shades of grey. When you appreciate what you do have and where you are, the colors begin to return. You begin to feel more abundant and secure. It makes easier to believe that you are actually doing okay irrespective of where you are right now, you can handle it. You have come this far and you can make things even better.

4. **The blissful fountain**

   Practice of gratitude helps you to experience more good feelings. When you appreciate something you feel good about, it leads to other positive feelings, such as, happiness, peace and joy. The better you feel, the easier it is overcome old patterns. Negative thoughts start to shrink down when you start feeling good. It starts a chain reaction. The more good feelings you have, the more optimistic you become. The more optimistic you become, the more opportunities and good things start to pour in. This empowers you with more things to be grateful for.

5. **Add miles to your memories**

   Practicing gratitude leads to happier memories. By taking the time to allow yourself to relax, you start to live in the present and fully experience all the wonder that your life has to offer you. You not only create a better present but you also create a storehouse of wonderful memories. If it seems that your life is full of bad memories, you can turn it around. One of the best ways to overcome old bad memories is to create a lot of new happy ones. Focus on making so many good memories that you do not have room for the old ones. Practice of gratitude is good way to start.

Practicing gratitude doesn't have to be done at a specific time or day. It can be done whenever and wherever is right for you. True gratitude is a state of mind, a way of feeling and perceiving what's in your life and in the entire Universe around you. This in itself is a lot to be grateful for.

Friends, 'gratitude is the sign of noble souls'. It takes a bit of work, but having an attitude of gratitude is one of the most impactful habits for a fulfilling and healthy life. Scientific research tells us that gratitude can change our lives and produces well being. When we train ourselves to look at life through the lens of gratitude rather than disappointment, we find ourselves happier and more at peace. Express gratitude while kindling the leader inside you and you would be surprised by the results. Practice the act of gratitude and live your life at full throttle, as a pioneer!

"Gratitude turns what we have into enough."

—Anonymous

In Conclusion

One of the reasons why mankind is where it is today is because great thinkers thought of the future and the challenges it holds. They envisaged the coming years and acted accordingly for which we have to be grateful. Yet, I have often realised that thinking of the future and worrying about it is exactly why none of us are ever able to have a good time with our present. It is also the precise reason why most of us find that years have gone by and we have done nothing to account for the past. Suddenly, one fine day you sit down and ask yourself, "What did I do all these years?" And then you worry some more.

You see, we are all intrinsically good people. We want the best for ourselves and our families and in the pursuit of that happiness we forget to live. Live and breathe and be thankful for what we have. I often travel the country talking to a variety of people about life and things in general. The usual questions crop up and I talk to them about this theory that I have been propagating for many years now. ***"The future is abstract"!!***

Many great minds are of the opinion that there is a tiny bit of possibility we can travel to the past, but travel to the future is not possible. It is simply because the past has happened and the future has not happened yet. What does that leave us with? Our present, of course! You see when today comes we have today's present and when tomorrow comes we have well, tomorrow's present. And this goes on every single day. Think of it in this way. The future is this huge brick wall you have to build over time. Every single day you are allowed to put just a single brick in that wall. Will you not put your best brick forward? And will you not make sure you make the best and strongest brick you can? Well there is your answer. ***If you desire to build a strong and robust wall, it is your job to put good bricks in that wall every single day.*** You really can't afford to put some good bricks, some bad ones and some really good ones again. And that is exactly how a good future works. Nothing but a huge collection of great 'presents' every day.

Enjoy your present, have fun, live well and put your best foot forward... Every day.

Think about it.

About the Author

Shridhar is one of India's most admired motivational speakers and is a leading authority on the application of sensible thinking for personal and organizational development. A popular speaker and story teller, he lectures to corporations, associations and universities in India and many other countries on leadership and capacity-building for organizational strategy. He is the founder of Curiosity Consulting and has lead seminars for organizations such as the Weichai Group, HSBC, Fiat India, DEIF and the Government of Tanzania. As a tactical and strategic organizational development specialist and change management expert, he has initiated several human resources and talent management strategic interventions. He brings more than 15 years of experience as a professional speaker, seminar leader and organizational consultant to his diverse, international clientele. He coaches present and future leaders and helps them to determine their desired behavior in their leadership roles.

Shridhar's passion for applying sensible thinking to personal and organizational development is also expressed in this book. He tries to introduce the concept of kindness in organizations for accelerated learning and team building. This is his first book and is the result of the myriad experiences of his life surfaced during the last 20 years of his career.

Shridhar loves to teach through the stories of his life. With only wit and humor for company, he has travelled more than ten countries to get a microscopic view of how humanities affect the way we live and create relationships. He loves to mix with local cultures and has had some great experiences. He once worked as a bartender for three months in the Seychelles mixing with the world's rich and the famous and believes that was the best education he ever received. In 2005, he stayed in Las Vegas for six months helping some friends set up a small business, spending time amongst the locals and learning from them.

In September 2011, he was part of a small research expedition which ended at the famous mystery skeleton lake of India, situated at 16000 feet in the Himalayas, also called as Roopkund.

He loves to listen, exercise, swim and read good fiction by the beach.

Shridhar lives in Pune, India with his wife and their daughter. He invites readers to email him at shridhar@curiosityconsulting.in or to visit his website at www.curiosityco.in

www.ingramcontent.com/pod-product-compliance
Lightning Source LLC
Chambersburg PA
CBHW050019170726
48282CB00025B/468
* 9 7 8 9 3 5 7 8 4 4 0 5 5 *